Cambridge Latin Course

INTEGRATED EDITION

Unit IIIA

with Language Information

CAMBRIDGE
UNIVERSITY PRESS

PUBLISHED BY THE PRESS SYNDICATE OF THE UNIVERSITY OF CAMBRIDGE
The Pitt Building, Trumpington Street, Cambridge CB2 1RP, United Kingdom

CAMBRIDGE UNIVERSITY PRESS
The Edinburgh Building, Cambridge CB2 2RU, United Kingdom
40 West 20th Street, New York, NY 10011–4211, USA
10 Stamford Road, Oakleigh, Melbourne 3166, Australia

This book, an outcome of work jointly commissioned by the Schools Council before its
closure and the Cambridge School Classics Project, is published under the aegis of
SCAA Enterprises Limited, Newcombe House, 45 Notting Hill Gate, London W11 3JB

First published 1972
Seventh printing 1982
Second edition 1983
Ninth printing 1989
Integrated Edition 1990
Eighth printing 1997

Printed in the United Kingdom at the University Press, Cambridge

ISBN 0 521 38948 8

DS

Cover picture: An onyx cameo of the Roman imperial eagle, engraved around AD 40.
(Kunsthistorisches Museum, Vienna).

Thanks are due to the following for permission to reproduce photographs:
pp.11, 21, 35, 57 Bath Museums Services; p.22 photograph by Bob Wilkins, copyright
Bath Archaeological Trust; pp.28, 79 (top) reproduced by courtesy of the Trustees of the
British Museum; p.54 Museo Civico, Piacenza; p.71 Cambridge University Collection,
copyright reserved; p.73 Rheinisches Landesmuseum Trier; p.79 (bottom) The Museum
of London; p.80 Rijksmuseum G.M. Kam; p.92 The Mansell Collection; p.108 (top), 125
The Grosvenor Museum, Chester; p.108 (bottom) copyright Verulamium Museum; p.141
Werner Forman Archive.

Map by Reg Piggott

Drawings by Peter Kesteven, Joy Mellor and Leslie Jones

Contents

Aquae Sūlis

in oppidō Aquīs Sūlis labōrābant multī fabrī, quī thermās maximās exstruēbant. architectus Rōmānus fabrōs īnspiciēbat.

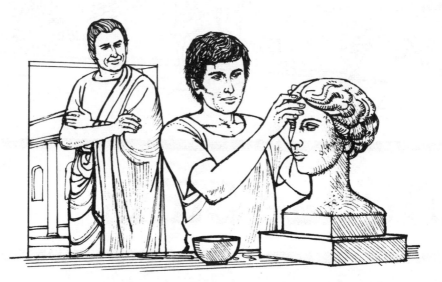

faber prīmus statuam deae Sūlis sculpēbat.
architectus fabrum laudāvit, quod perītus erat et dīligenter labōrābat.
faber, ab architectō laudātus, laetissimus erat.

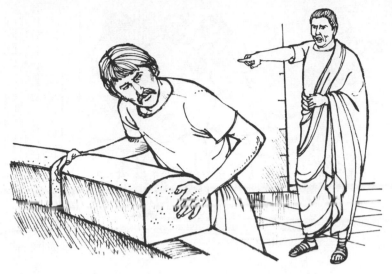

faber secundus mūrum circum fontem pōnēbat.
architectus fabrum incitāvit, quod fessus erat et lentē labōrābat.
faber, ab architectō incitātus, rem graviter ferēbat. nihil tamen
dīxit, quod architectum timēbat.

faber tertius aquam ad balneum ē fonte sacrō portābat.
architectus fabrum vituperāvit, quod ignāvus erat et minimē
labōrābat.
faber, ab architectō vituperātus, īnsolenter respondit.

architectus, ubi verba īnsolentia fabrī audīvit, servōs suōs arcessīvit.

servī, ab architectō arcessītī, fabrum comprehendērunt et in balneum dēiēcērunt.

'linguam sordidam habēs', inquit architectus cachinnāns. 'melius est tibi aquam sacram bibere.'

fōns sacer

Quīntus apud Salvium manēbat per tōtam hiemem. saepe ad aulam Cogidubnī ībat, ā rēge invītātus. Quīntus eī multa dē vītā suā nārrābat, quod rēx aliquid novī audīre semper volēbat.

ubi vēr appropinquābat, Cogidubnus in morbum gravem incidit. multī medicī, ad aulam arcessītī, remedium morbī quaesīvērunt. 5
ingravēscēbat tamen morbus. rēx Quīntum et Salvium dē remediō anxius cōnsuluit.

'mī Quīnte', inquit, 'tū es vir magnae prūdentiae. volō tē mihi cōnsilium dare. ad fontem sacrum īre dēbeō?'

fōns *fountain, spring*
aliquid novī *something new*
morbum: morbus *illness*
gravem: gravis *serious*
cōnsuluit: cōnsulere *consult*
vir magnae prūdentiae *a man of great prudence, a man of good sense*
cōnsilium *advice*

'ubi est iste fōns?' rogāvit Quīntus.   10

'est in oppidō Aquīs Sūlis', respondit Cogidubnus. 'multī aegrōtī,
quī ex hōc fonte aquam bibērunt, posteā convaluērunt. architectum
Rōmānum illūc mīsī, quī thermās maximās exstrūxit. prope
thermās stat templum deae Sūlis, ā meīs fabrīs aedificātum. ego
deam saepe honōrāvī; nunc fortasse dea mē sānāre potest. Salvī, tū 15
es vir magnae calliditātis; volō tē mihi cōnsilium dare. quid facere
dēbeō?'

'tū es vir sapiēns', respondit ille. 'melius est tibi testāmentum
facere.'

oppidō: oppidum *town*
Aquīs Sūlis: Aquae Sūlis *Bath*
aegrōtī: aegrōtus *invalid*
convaluērunt: convalēscere *get better, recover*
exstrūxit: exstruere *build*
calliditātis: calliditās *cleverness, shrewdness*

When you have read section I of this story, answer the questions at the end of the section.

Lūcius Marcius Memor

I

oppidum Aquae Sūlis parvum erat, thermae maximae. prōcūrātor thermārum erat Lūcius Marcius Memor, nōtissimus haruspex, homō obēsus et ignāvus. quamquam iam tertia hōra erat, Memor in cubiculō ēbrius dormiēbat. Cephalus, haruspicis lībertus, Memorem excitāre temptābat.   5

prōcūrātor *manager*
haruspex *soothsayer*
obēsus *fat*

'domine! domine!' clāmābat.

haruspex, graviter dormiēns, nihil respondit.

'dominus nimium vīnī rūrsus bibit', sibi dīxit lībertus. 'domine! surge! hōra tertia est.'

Memor, ā lībertō tandem excitātus, ūnum oculum aperuit.   10

'fer mihi plūs vīnī!' inquit. 'tum abī!'

'domine! domine! necesse est tibi surgere', inquit Cephalus.

'cūr mē vexās, Cephale?' respondit Memor. 'cūr tū rem administrāre ipse nōn potes?'

'rem huius modī administrāre nōn possum', respondit lībertus.   15
'sunt multī servī, multī fabrī, quī mandāta prōcūrātōris exspectant.
tē exspectat architectus ipse, vir magnae dignitātis. tē exspectant
aegrōtī. adstant sacerdōtēs parātī. adsunt mercātōrēs, quōs
arcessīvistī. tū rem ipse administrāre dēbēs.'

'numquam dēsinit labor', clāmāvit Memor. 'quam fessus sum!   20
cūr ad hunc populum barbarum umquam vēnī?'

Cephalus, quī rīsum cēlāre temptābat, Memorī respondit,

'haruspex callidissimus es. nōnne aegrōtīs remedia praebēre vīs?
nōnne Britannīs mōrēs Rōmānōs impōnere vīs?'

'es homō magnae stultitiae', respondit Memor. 'aegrōtōs floccī   25
nōn faciō. Britannōs etiam minōris pretiī habeō. sed nunc mihi
commodum est hoc tam molestum officium agere. sīc enim ad
maiōrēs honōrēs ascendere possum. ego virōs potentēs colere velim.
ēheu! in hāc īnsulā sunt paucī virī potentēs, paucī clārī.'

'quid vīs mē facere, Memor?' rogāvit lībertus.   30

'iubeō tē omnēs dīmittere', clāmāvit Memor. 'nōlī mē iterum
vexāre!'

Memor, postquam haec verba dīxit, statim obdormīvit.
Cephalus, ā dominō īrātō territus, invītus exiit. extrā cubiculum
multitūdinem aegrōtōrum invēnit, Memorem exspectantium et   35
vehementer clāmantium. inter aegrōtōs erant nōnnūllī mīlitēs, ab
hostibus nūper vulnerātī et paene interfectī. adstābant quoque
multī fabrī, Memorem absentem vituperantēs. eōs omnēs Cephalus
dīmīsit.

graviter *heavily, soundly*
nimium vīnī *too much wine*
rūrsus *again*
fer! *bring!*
plūs vīnī *more wine*
huius modī *of this kind*
mandāta *instructions, orders*
dignitātis: dignitās *importance, prestige*
adstant: adstāre *stand by*
dēsinit: dēsinere *end, cease*
labor *work*
populum: populus *people*
umquam *ever*
rīsum: rīsus *smile*
praebēre *provide*
mōrēs: mōs *custom*

impōnere *impose*
stultitiae: stultitia *stupidity*
etiam minōris pretiī habeō *I care even
  less about*
officium *duty*
sīc *in this way*
honōrēs: honor *honour*
potentēs: potens *powerful*
colere *seek favour of, make friends with*
velim *I should like*
clārī: clārus *famous, distinguished*
haec verba *these words*
territus: terrēre *frighten*
hostibus: hostis *enemy*
absentem: absēns *absent*

1 What is the time of day at the start of this story? What is Memor's freedman trying to do?
2 What does the word 'rūrsus' (line 8) suggest about Memor's habits?
3 How many different groups and individuals are waiting to see Memor, according to Cephalus (lines 16–18)?
4 Why does Cephalus say 'mandāta prōcūrātōris' (line 16) rather than 'mandāta tua'?
5 What do you think makes Cephalus smile (line 22)? Why does he try to hide the smile?
6 According to Cephalus (lines 23–4), what were Memor's reasons for coming to work at Bath? Does Cephalus mean this seriously?
7 According to Memor himself (lines 27–8), what was his real reason for coming to Bath? Why has he found it hard to achieve what he wanted?
8 In line 31, Memor says 'iubeō tē omnēs dīmittere'. Which words in the last paragraph tell you that this order was obeyed?

II

mox tamen, Cephalus cubiculum rūrsus intrāvit Memoremque
dormientem excitāvit. Memor, simulac Cephalum vīdit, īrātus
clāmāvit,
'cūr prohibēs mē dormīre? cūr mihi nōn pārēs? stultior es quam
asinus.'   5
'sed domine', respondit Cephalus, 'aliquid novī nūntiāre volō.
postquam hinc discessī, mandāta, quae mihi dedistī, effēcī. ubi
tamen aegrōtōs fabrōsque dīmittēbam, senātōrem thermīs
appropinquantem cōnspexī.'
'quis est ille senātor?' rogāvit Memor, valdē vexātus. 'unde vēnit? 1(
senātōrem vidēre nōlō.'
'melius est tibi hunc senātōrem vidēre', respondit Cephalus.
'nam Gāius Salvius est.'
'num Gāius Salvius Līberālis?' exclāmāvit Memor. 'nōn crēdō
tibi.'   1!
Cephalus tamen facile eī persuāsit, quod Salvius iam in āream
thermārum equitābat.
Memor perterritus statim clāmāvit,
'fer mihi togam! fer calceōs! ōrnāmenta mea ubi sunt? vocā
servōs! quam īnfēlīx sum! Salvius hūc venit, vir summae 2(
auctōritātis, quem colere maximē volō.'
Memor celerrimē togam calceōsque induit. Cephalus eī
ōrnāmenta trādidit, ex armāriō raptim extracta. haruspex lībertum
innocentem vituperābat, lībertus Salvium.

prohibēs: prohibēre *prevent*
hinc *from here*
effēcī: efficere *carry out, accomplish*
calceōs: calceus *shoe*
ōrnāmenta *decorations*
auctōritātis: auctōritās *authority*
raptim *hastily, quickly*

Base of a statue dedicated to the goddess Sulis by Lucius Marcius Memor

About the language

1   In Stage 20, you met sentences like these, containing *present* participles:

servī per vīllam contendērunt, arāneās **quaerentēs**.
The slaves hurried through the house, looking for spiders' webs.

astrologus, amulētum **tenēns**, ad nōs accurrit.
The astrologer, holding an amulet, ran up to us.

2   In Stage 21, you have met sentences like these:

Memor, ā lībertō **excitātus**, īrātissimus erat.
Memor, having been awakened by the freedman, was very angry.

templum, ā fabrīs perītīs **ōrnātum**, splendidissimum erat.
The temple, having been decorated by skilful craftsmen, was very impressive.

The words in heavy print are *perfect* participles.

3   A perfect participle is used to describe a noun. For instance, in the first example in paragraph 2, 'excitātus' describes Memor.

4   Translate the following examples:

1 servus, ā dominō verberātus, ē vīllā fūgit.
2 saltātrīx, ā spectātōribus laudāta, rīsit.
3 nūntius, ad rēgem arcessītus, rem terribilem nārrāvit.

Pick out the perfect participle in each sentence and find the noun which it describes.

5   A perfect participle changes its ending to agree with the noun it describes. For example:

singular fūr, ā centuriōne superātus, veniam petīvit.
plural   fūrēs, ā centuriōne superātī, veniam petīvērunt.

6 Translate the following examples and pick out the perfect participle in each sentence:

1 senex, ab astrologō monitus, nāvigāre nōluit.
2 prīncipēs, ā rēge vocātī, celeriter ad aulam vēnērunt.
3 cēna, ā coquō Graecō parāta, omnēs hospitēs dēlectāvit.

Find the noun which each perfect participle is describing and say whether each noun-and-participle pair is singular or plural.

7 There are two kinds of perfect participle in Latin. The one described in this Stage is known as the *perfect passive* participle. You will meet the other kind in Stage 22.

8 Notice two different ways of translating perfect passive participles:

architectus, ā Cogidubnō ipsō missus, thermās maximās exstrūxit.
The architect, having been sent by Cogidubnus himself, built some very large baths.
  or, in more natural English,
The architect, sent by Cogidubnus himself, built some very large baths.

mercātōrēs, ā latrōnibus graviter vulnerātī, in fossā iacēbant.
The merchants, having been seriously wounded by robbers, were lying in the ditch.
The merchants, seriously wounded by robbers, were lying in the ditch.

Memor rem suscipit

Salvius et Memor, in hortō sōlī ambulantēs, sermōnem gravem habent.

Salvius: Lūcī Marcī Memor, vir summae prūdentiae es. volō tē
rem magnam suscipere.

Memor: tālem rem suscipere velim, sed occupātissimus sum.
exspectant mē aegrōtī et sacerdōtēs. vexant mē 5
architectus et fabrī. sed quid vīs mē facere?

Salvius: Tiberius Claudius Cogidubnus, rēx Rēgnēnsium, hūc
nūper advēnit. Cogidubnus, quī in morbum gravem
incidit, aquam ē fonte sacrō bibere vult.

Memor: difficile est mihi tē adiuvāre, mī senātor. Cogidubnus est 10
vir octōgintā annōrum. difficile est deae Sūlī Cogidubnum sānāre.

Salvius: nōlō tē reddere Cogidubnum sānum. volō tē rem
contrāriam efficere.

Memor: quid dīcis? num mortem Cogidubnī cupis?   15
Salvius: ita vērō! porrō, quamquam tam occupātus es, volō tē
ipsum hanc rem efficere.

Memor: vīsne mē mortem eī parāre? rem huius modī facere nōn
ausim. Cogidubnus enim est vir clārissimus, ā populō
Rōmānō honōrātus.   20

Salvius: es vir summae calliditātis. hanc rem efficere potes. nōn
sōlum ego, sed etiam Imperātor, hoc cupit. Cogidubnus
enim Rōmānōs saepe vexāvit. Imperātor mihi, nōn
Cogidubnō, cōnfīdit. Imperātor tibi praemium dignum
prōmittit. num praemium recūsāre vīs, tibi ab 25
Imperātōre prōmissum?

Memor: quō modō id facere possum?
Salvius: nescio. hoc tantum tibi dīcō: Imperātor mortem
Cogidubnī exspectat.

Memor: ō mē miserum! rem difficiliōrem numquam fēcī.   30
Salvius: vīta, mī Memor, est plēna rērum difficilium.
(exit Salvius.)

Memor: Cephale! Cephale! (*lībertus, ā Memore vocātus, celeriter intrat. pōculum vīnī fert.*) cūr mihi vīnum offers? nōn vīnum, sed cōnsilium quaerō. iubeō tē mihi cōnsilium 35 quam celerrimē dare. rēx Cogidubnus hūc vēnit, remedium morbī petēns. Imperātor, ā Cogidubnō saepe vexātus, iam mortem eius cupit. Imperātor ipse iubet mē hoc efficere. quam difficile est!

Cephalus: minimē, facile est! pōculum venēnātum habeō, mihi ā 40 latrōne Aegyptiō ōlim datum. venēnum, in pōculō cēlātum, vītam celerrimē exstinguere potest.

Memor: cōnsilium, quod mihi prōpōnis, perīculōsum est. Cogidubnō venēnum dare timeō.

Cephalus: nihil perīculī est. rēx, quotiēns ē balneō exiit, ad fontem 45 deae īre solet. tum necesse est servō prope fontem deae stāre et pōculum rēgī offerre.

Memor: (*dēlectātus*) cōnsilium optimum est. nūllīs tamen servīs cōnfīdere ausim. sed tibi cōnfīdō, Cephale. iubeō tē ipsum Cogidubnō pōculum offerre. 50

Cephalus: ēheu! vīta lībertī dūra est. mihi rem difficillimam impōnis.

Memor: vīta, mī Cephale, est plēna rērum difficilium.

tālem: tālis *such*	nescio: nescīre *not know*
octoginta *eighty*	venēnātum: venēnātus *poisoned*
reddere *make*	datum: dare *give*
sānum: sānus *well, healthy*	venēnum *poison*
rem contrāriam: rēs contrāria	exstinguere *extinguish, destroy*
the opposite	prōpōnis: prōpōnere *propose, put forward*
porrō *what's more, furthermore*	nihil perīculī *no danger*
nōn ausim *I shouldn't dare*	quotiēns *whenever*
nōn sōlum . . . sed etiam *not only*	balneō: balneum *bath*
. . . *but also*	difficillimam: difficillimus *very difficult*
dignum: dignus *worthy, appropriate*	

About the language

1   Study the following examples:

> plūs cibī   more food
> nimium vīnī   too much wine

Each example is made up of two words:

1 a word like 'plūs' or 'nimium' which indicates an *amount* or *quantity*,
2 a noun in the *genitive* case.

2   Further examples:

> satis pecūniae   nimium perīculī
> nimium cibī   plūs sanguinis
> plūs labōris   satis aquae

Practising the language

1   Study the form and meaning of the following words, and give the meaning of the untranslated ones:

laetus	happy	laetē	happily
perītus	skilful	perītē	skilfully
stultissimus	very foolish	stultissimē	very foolishly
tacitus	silent	tacitē	
cautus	cautious	cautē	
probus		probē	honestly
callidus		callidē	cleverly, cunningly
superbus	proud	superbē	
crūdēlissimus	very cruel	crūdēlissimē	
sevērissimus	very severe	sevērissimē	
līberālissimus		līberālissimē	very generously

The words in the left-hand pair of columns are *adjectives*. Adjectives were described in Stage 14 and the Language Information sections of Units IIA and IIB.

The words in the right-hand pair of columns are known as *adverbs*.

Give the meaning of the following adverbs:

intentē, firmē, stultē, saevē, dīligentissimē

2 Complete each sentence with the right word and then translate.

1 omnēs aegrōtī . . . . . vīsitāre volēbant. (fōns, fontem, fontis)
2 plūrimī servī in fundō . . . . . labōrābant. (dominus, dominum, dominī)
3 'fortasse . . . . . morbum meum sānāre potest', inquit rēx. (dea, deam, deae)
4 . . . . . Cogidubnum laudāvērunt, quod līberālis et sapiēns erat. (prīncipēs, prīncipum)
5 mercātor, postquam . . . . . in saccō posuit, ē forō discessit. (dēnāriī, dēnāriōs, dēnāriōrum)
6 senex, quī in Arabiā diū habitāverat, magnum numerum . . . . . collēgerat. (gemmae, gemmās, gemmārum)

3 Complete each sentence with the right word from the list below and then translate.

parāvī, rapuērunt, amīcōrum, hastam, nūntius, hospitibus

1 puer, in cubiculō dormiēns, vōcēs . . . . . nōn audīvit.
2 'optimam cēnam tibi . . . . ., domine', inquit coquus.
3 senex, quī avārus erat, ... vīnum offerre nōlēbat.
4 in rīpā flūminis stābat servus, quī . . . . . in manibus tenēbat.
5 subitō latrōnēs irrūpērunt et pecūniam . . . . . .
6 . . . . ., quem rēx mīserat, epistulam in itinere āmīsit.

4 Translate each English sentence into Latin by selecting correctly from the pairs of Latin words.

For example: The messenger heard the voice of the old man.

        nūntius   vōcem   senem   audīvī
        nūntium   vōcī   senis   audīvit

Answer: nūntius vōcem senis audīvit.

1 The priests showed the statue to the architect.

    sacerdōtēs   statuam architectum   ostendit
    sacerdōtibus statuās architectō   ostendērunt

2 The king praised the skilful doctor.

    rēx   medicus   perītum   laudāvit
    rēgēs   medicum   perītī   laudāvērunt

3 A friend of the soldiers was visiting the temple.

    amīcus   mīlitis   templum vīsitābat
    amīcō   mīlitum templī   vīsitāvit

4 The shouts of the invalids had annoyed the soothsayer.

    clāmōrem   aegrōtī   haruspicem vexāverant
    clāmōrēs   aegrōtōrum haruspicēs vexāvērunt

5 We handed over the master's money to the farmers.

    pecūnia   dominum agricolās trādidimus
    pecūniam dominī   agricolīs trādidērunt

5 Complete each sentence with the right word and then translate.

1 tū ipse hanc rem administrāre . . . . . .(dēbeō, dēbēs, dēbet)

2 'domine! surge!' clāmāvit Cephalus. 'nam Gāius Salvius thermīs . . . . . .' (appropinquō, appropinquās, appropinquat)

3 cūr mē vituperās? heri per tōtum diem . . . . . . (labōrāvī, labōrāvistī, labōrāvit)

4 ego, quod fontem sacrum vidēre . . . . ., iter ad oppidum Aquās Sūlis fēcī. (cupiēbam, cupiēbās, cupiēbat)

5 lībertus, quī senātōrem . . . . ., in cubiculum haruspicis ruit. (cōnspexeram, cōnspexerās, cōnspexerat)

6 ubi poēta versum scurrīlem recitāvit, amīcus meus īrātus erat; ego tamen . . . . . . (rīsī, rīsistī, rīsit)

7 ē lectō surrēxī, quod dormīre nōn . . . . . . (poteram, poterās, poterat)

8 in hāc vīllā . . . . . Memor, haruspex nōtissimus. (habitō, habitās, habitat)

Aquae Sulis and its baths

The modern city of Bath lies in the valley of the river Avon, just to the east of Bristol. In a small area of low-lying ground, enclosed by a bend in the river, mineral springs of hot water emerge from underground at the rate of over a million litres (a quarter of a million gallons) a day. The water has a temperature of between 40 and 49 degrees centigrade (104 and 121 degrees fahrenheit). It has a low mineral content (calcium, magnesium and sodium are the main minerals) and microscopic traces of radium. It was here that the Celts who lived in the surrounding hills came to worship the goddess of the spring, Sulis, long before the Romans arrived in Britain. The Celts clearly recognised the power of the goddess to produce hot water from the ground, but they also saw the power of the goddess in the healing properties of the spring water.

As Roman settlers moved gradually westwards after the invasion of A.D. 43, they soon brought changes to the region. Much of the rich farmland owned by Celtic farmers was taken over and turned into villa estates in the Roman style. The Romans recognised that the springs of Sulis were an important religious centre and they erected huge public baths and other buildings so that visitors might enjoy the healing properties of the hot mineral waters in comfort. No doubt the heat helped relieve conditions such as rheumatism and arthritis, but many people must have visited the baths in the hope of miraculous cures for all kinds of diseases. During the latter part of the first century A.D. the new Romano-British town of Aquae Sulis began to grow up. The Roman writer, Pliny the Elder, said in his *Natural History*: 'Healing springs help to encourage the growth of towns' and Aquae Sulis was no exception. The healing springs, a mild climate and a sheltered position were all reasons why the town developed as an important spa.

The Roman masons had good supplies of limestone quarried locally, and the nearby Mendip Hills provided the lead needed for lining the baths. The main building was a long, rectangular structure, larger and more magnificent than any other set of baths west of Rome at this date. It contained three main plunge baths filled with a constant supply of water at a pleasant temperature. The water was brought from the hot spring through lead pipes. The pool nearest the spring naturally contained the hottest water, whereas the furthest pool was the coolest, since the water lost much of its heat on the way to it. To provide a focal point for visitors to the baths, the Romans surrounded the spring with a lead-lined reservoir some 12–15 metres (40–50 feet) across. At a later date, they built a viewing platform and roofed the entire structure.

Temple and baths at Aquae Sulis (1st century A.D.)

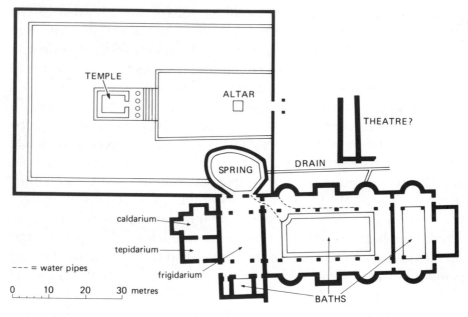

Aquae Sulis lay within tribal territory over which Cogidubnus may have had control. It is just possible that he himself was responsible for or at least had a hand in the development of the town. This building project certainly matched the splendour of the palace at Fishbourne which was erected at about the same time.

At the time of our story (A.D. 83), Aquae Sulis was a small but growing community. The bath buildings were still being erected but were already the most impressive feature of the town. There were probably a few other public buildings, such as a 'basilica' (hall) for the administration of law and local government, and possibly a theatre, but most of the other buildings would have been houses for those who had already made their home in the town, and inns for the town's many visitors.

Some people travelled long distances to Aquae Sulis, attracted by the fame of its spring and hoping that the healing power of the waters would cure their illnesses. One elderly woman, Rusonia Aventina, came from Metz in eastern Gaul. Her tombstone shows that she died at Aquae Sulis at the age of fifty-eight, perhaps from the illness which she had hoped the spring would cure. Julius Vitalis was a soldier serving as armourer to the Twentieth Legion, based at Chester. His tombstone shows that he had served for just nine years

The Great Bath

when he died at the age of twenty-nine; possibly his commanding officer had sent him to Aquae Sulis on sick leave. But many visitors came and departed in good health.

The Roman authorities were quick to realise that Aquae Sulis was becoming a popular place of pilgrimage. Visitors entering the new bath buildings and seeing the mysterious hot waters bubbling in the newly built reservoir would feel that they were entering a holy place. They thought that a cure for their ailments depended as much on divine favour as on the medicinal powers of the water. A temple was therefore constructed next to the bath buildings and dedicated to the goddess Sulis Minerva. By linking the two names in this way, the Romans encouraged the British people to worship Minerva, goddess of healing and the arts, together with their own goddess, Sulis. The temple stood in a specially enclosed area, with a

Inscribed pewter and silver bowls thrown as offerings into the sacred spring

magnificent altar in front and a bronze statue of the goddess inside.

The appointment of a Roman official, Lucius Marcius Memor, to take charge of the religious activities at Aquae Sulis is another example of the Romans' efforts to spread Roman ways and customs among the Britons. In the story on page 8 he complains of having to live and work in Britain, but he reluctantly accepts that this is necessary if he is to further his career back in Rome. Clearly, Memor has been posted to the province of Britain to help promote the Roman way of life. Many such officials must have contributed to the policy of 'romanisation' in this way.

Aquae Sulis was, of course, something of a tourist centre as well as a place of religious pilgrimage, and one can imagine the entrance to the baths crowded with souvenir stalls and sellers of lucky charms. Visitors would often buy such offerings to throw into the sacred spring with a prayer for future good health. These offerings were sometimes expensive: they included, for example, beautifully carved gemstones and other items of jewellery.

The full extent of the bath and temple buildings is only gradually becoming known to us from the work of archaeologists. The most recent excavations have revealed the details of construction of the Roman reservoir surrounding the hot spring itself, and important work was carried out in 1982 on the temple precinct. The results of these excavations are on display in the museum. Many thousands of Roman coins have been recovered from the spring, together with silver and pewter vessels thrown in as offerings to the goddess. About fifty small sheets of lead or pewter were also found with Latin inscriptions on them. Their translations show that some people were anxious to use the powers of Sulis Minerva for more sinister purposes than good health, as we shall see in Stage 22.

Words and phrases checklist

From now on, most verbs in the checklists are listed as in the Unit IIIA Language Information section (i.e. perfect passive participles are usually included).

ā, ab – by
adiuvō, adiuvāre, adiūvī – help
annus, annī – year
ascendō, ascendere, ascendī – climb, rise
barbarus, barbarī – barbarian
cēlō, cēlāre, cēlāvī, cēlātus – hide
circum – around
cōnfīdō, cōnfīdere – trust
dēiciō, dēicere, dēiēcī, dēiectus – throw down
dūrus, dūra, dūrum – harsh, hard
efficiō, efficere, effēcī, effectus – carry out, accomplish
extrahō, extrahere, extrāxī, extractus – drag out, pull out
fōns, fontis – fountain, spring
gravis, grave – heavy, serious
haruspex, haruspicis – soothsayer
hōra, hōrae – hour
īnfēlīx, *gen.* īnfēlīcis – unlucky
iubeō, iubēre, iussī, iussus – order
morbus, morbī – illness
nōnnūllī, nōnnūllae – some, several
nūper – recently
occupātus, occupāta, occupātum – busy
oppidum, oppidī – town
perītus, perīta, perītum – skilful
plēnus, plēna, plēnum – full
plūs, *gen.* plūris – more
pretium, pretiī – price
sapiēns, *gen.* sapientis – wise
suscipiō, suscipere, suscēpī, susceptus – undertake, take on
unde – from where

dēfīxiō

fūr thermīs cautē
appropinquāvit.
fūr, thermās ingressus, ad
fontem sacrum festīnāvit.

fūr, prope fontem stāns,
circumspectāvit.
fūr, senem cōnspicātus, post
columnam sē cēlāvit.

senex, amulētum aureum tenēns,
ad fontem prōcessit.
senex oculōs ad caelum sustulit
et deae Sūlī precēs adhibuit.

senex, deam precātus, amulētum
in fontem iniēcit et exiit.

fūr, quī amulētum aureum
vīderat, ad fontem iterum
festīnāvit.
fūr, ad fontem regressus,
amulētum in aquā quaesīvit.

fūr, amulētum adeptus, attonitus lēgit:

fūr amulētum dēiēcit et ē thermīs perterritus fūgit.

27

Vilbia

Vilbia et Rubria, pōcula sordida lavantēs, in culīnā tabernae garriēbant. hae puellae erant fīliae Latrōnis. Latrō, quī tabernam tenēbat, erat vir magnae dīligentiae sed minimae prūdentiae. Latrō, culīnam ingressus, puellās castīgābat.

'multa sunt pōcula sordida. iubeō vōs pōcula quam celerrimē 5 lavāre. labōrāte! nōlīte garrīre! loquāciōrēs estis quam psittacī.'

Latrō, haec verba locūtus, exiit.

Vilbia, tamen, quae pulchra et obstināta erat, patrem floccī nōn faciēbat. pōcula nōn lāvit, sed Rubriae fībulam ostendit. Rubria fībulam, quam soror tenēbat, avidē spectāvit.   1

Rubria: quam pulchra, quam pretiōsa est haec fībula, mea Vilbia! eam īnspicere velim. quis tibi dedit? num argentea est?

Vilbia: sānē argentea est. Modestus, mīles Rōmānus, eam mihi dedit.

Rubria: quālis est hic mīles? estne homō mendāx, sīcut cēterī 1 mīlitēs Rōmānī? multī mīlitēs vulnera fingunt, quod perīcula bellī vītāre volunt. Modestus quoque ignāvus est?

Vilbia: minimē! est vir maximae virtūtis. ōlim tria mīlia hostium occīdit. nunc lēgātum ipsum custōdit.

Rubria: Herculēs alter est! ego autem tālēs fābulās saepe ex aliīs 2(mīlitibus audīvī.

Vilbia: cēterī mīlitēs mendācēs sunt, Modestus probus. Modestus hūc vēnit aeger. Modestus, in thermās ingressus, aquam sacram bibit. Modestus, deam Sūlem precātus, statim convaluit.   2.

Rubria: dissentīre nōn ausim. quō modō huic tam mīrābilī mīlitī occurristī?

Vilbia: simulac tabernam nostram intrāvit Modestus, eum statim amāvī. quantī erant lacertī eius! quanta bracchia!

Rubria: tibi favet fortūna, mea Vilbia. quid autem dē Bulbō dīcis, 3(quem ōlim amābās? tibi perīculōsum est Bulbum contemnere, quod rēs magicās intellegit.

Vilbia: nōlī illam pestem commemorāre! Bulbus, saepe dē
mātrimōniō locūtus, nihil umquam effēcit. sed Modestus,
quī fortissimus et audācissimus est, mē cūrāre potest. 35
Modestus nunc est suspīrium meum.

dīligentiae: dīligentia *industry, hard work*
minimae: minimus *very little*
ingressus *having entered*
locūtus *having spoken*
fībulam: fībula *brooch*
avidē *eagerly*
quālis? *what sort of man?*
vulnera fingunt *pretend to be wounded, invent wounds*
bellī: bellum *war*
virtūtis: virtūs *courage*
tria mīlia *three thousand*
occīdit: occīdere *kill*
lēgātum: lēgātus *commander*
alter *another, a second*
autem *but*
precātus *having prayed to*
huic *this (dative of* hic)
occurristī: occurrere *meet*
quantī: quantus *how big*
lacertī: lacertus *muscle*
bracchia *arms*
contemnere *reject, despise*
mātrimōniō: mātrimōnium *marriage*
suspīrium *heart-throb*

Modestus

Modestus et Strȳthiō ad tabernam Latrōnis ambulant. Strȳthiō, quamquam amīcus Modestī est, eum dērīdet.

Modestus: ubi es, Strȳthiō? iubeō tē prope mē stāre.
Strȳthiō: adsum. hercle! quam fortūnātus sum! prope virum summae virtūtis sum. tū enim fortior es quam Mārs ipse.
Modestus: vērum dīcis. ōlim tria mīlia hostium occīdī.
Strȳthiō: tē omnēs puellae amant, quod tam fortis et pulcher es. illa Vilbia, heri tē cōnspicāta, statim amāvit. multa dē tē rogāvit.
Modestus: quid dīxit?
Strȳthiō: mē avidē rogāvit, 'estne Herculēs?' 'minimē! est frāter eius', respondī. tum fībulam, quam puella alia tibi dederat, Vilbiae trādidī. 'Modestus, vir benignus et nōbilis', inquam, 'tibi hanc fībulam grātīs dat.' Vilbia, fībulam adepta, mihi respondit, 'quam pulcher Modestus est! quam līberālis! velim cum eō colloquium habēre.'
Modestus: ēheu! nōnne molestae sunt puellae? mihi difficile est puellās vītāre. nimis pulcher sum.
Strȳthiō: ecce! ad tabernam Latrōnis advēnimus. fortasse inest Vilbia, quae tē tamquam deum adōrat.
(tabernam intrant.)

Mārs *Mars (god of war)*
vērum *the truth*
cōnspicāta: cōnspicātus *having caught sight of*
inquam *I said*
grātīs *free*
adepta: adeptus *having received, having obtained*
colloquium *talk, chat*
nimis *too*
inest: inesse *be inside*
tamquam *as, like*

About the language

1 In Stage 21 you met sentences containing *perfect passive* participles:

rēx, ā Rōmānīs **honōrātus**, semper fidēlis manēbat.
The king, having been honoured by the Romans, always remained loyal.

puerī, ā custōde **monitī**, ad vīllam rediērunt.
The boys, having been warned by the guard, returned to the house.

2 In Stage 22, you have met another kind of perfect participle. Study the way it is translated in the following examples:

Vilbia, culīnam **ingressa**, sorōrī fībulam ostendit.
Vilbia, having entered the kitchen, showed the brooch to her sister.

senex, haec verba **locūtus**, abiit.
The old man, having said these words, went away.

This kind of participle is a *perfect active* participle.

3 Translate the following examples and pick out the perfect active participle in each sentence:

1 iuvenis, ad thermās regressus, amīcum quaesīvit.
2 puellae, leōnem cōnspicātae, ad vīllam statim ruērunt.
3 mercātōrēs, pecūniam adeptī, ad nāvēs contendērunt.
4 ancilla, deam precāta, ā templō discessit.

Find the noun which each participle is describing.

amor omnia vincit

scaena prīma

Bulbus et amīcus in tabernā Latrōnis sunt. vīnum bibunt āleamque lūdunt.
Bulbus amīcō multam pecūniam dēbet.

Gutta (*amīcus Bulbī*): quam īnfēlīx es! nōn sōlum puellam, sed etiam
    pecūniam āmīsistī.

Bulbus: pecūniam floccī nōn faciō, sed puellam, quam maximē
    amō, āmittere nōlō.

Gutta: quō modō eam retinēre potes? mīles Rōmānus, vir summae
    virtūtis, eam petit. heus! Venerem iactāvī! caupō! iubeō tē
    plūs vīnī ferre.

Bulbus: mīles, quī eam dēcēpit, homō mendāx, prāvus, ignāvus est.
    Vilbia, ab eō dēcepta, nunc mē contemnit. eam saepe
    monuī, 'nōlī mīlitibus crēdere, praesertim Rōmānīs.'
    Vilbia tamen, hunc Modestum cōnspicāta, statim eum
    amāvit.

Gutta: puellīs nōn tūtum est per viās huius oppidī īre. tanta est
    arrogantia hōrum mīlitum. hercle! tū etiam īnfēlīcior es.
    canem iterum iactāvistī. alium dēnārium mihi dēbēs.

Bulbus: dēnārium libenter trādō, nōn puellam. ōdī istum mīlitem.
Modestus tamen puellam retinēre nōn potest, quod
auxilium ā deā petīvī. thermās ingressus, tabulam in 20
fontem sacrum iniēcī. dīra imprecātiō, in tabulā scrīpta,
iam in fonte deae iacet. (*intrant Modestus et Strȳthiō.*) exitium
Modestī laetus exspectō. nihil mihi obstāre potest.

Gutta: hercle! īnfēlīcissimus es. ecce! nōbīs appropinquat ipse
Modestus. necesse est mihi quam celerrimē exīre. 25
(*exit currēns.*)

amor *love*
omnia *all, everything*
scaena *scene*
āleam . . . lūdunt *are playing dice*
Venerem: Venus *Venus (highest throw at dice)*
iactāvī: iactāre *throw*
praesertim *especially*
arrogantia *cheek, arrogance*
canem: canis *dog (lowest throw at dice)*
ōdī *I hate*
tabulam: tabula *tablet, writing-tablet*
imprecātiō *curse*
scrīpta: scrībere *write*
exitium *ruin, destruction*

scaena secunda

Modestus īrātus Bulbum vituperat, quod verba eius audīvit.

Modestus: quid dīcēbās, homuncule? exitium meum exspectās? asine! tū, quod mīlitem Rōmānum vituperāvistī, in magnō perīculō es. mihi facile est tē, tamquam hostem, dīlaniāre. Strȳthiō! tē iubeō hanc pestem verberāre. 5 postquam eum verberāvistī, ē tabernā ēice!

Strȳthiō invītus Bulbum verberāre incipit. Bulbus, fortiter sē dēfendēns, vīnum in caput Strȳthiōnis fundit. Modestus Bulbum, simulac tergum vertit, ferōciter pulsat. Bulbus exanimātus prōcumbit. Vilbia, quae clāmōrēs audīvit, intrat. ingressa, Bulbum humī iacentem videt et Modestum mollīre incipit. 1

Vilbia: dēsine, mī Modeste. iste Bulbus, ā tē verberātus, iterum mē vexāre nōn potest. tū es leō, iste rīdiculus mūs. volō tē clēmentem esse et Bulbō parcere. placetne tibi?

Modestus: mihi placet. victōribus decōrum est victīs parcere. tē, nōn istum, quaerō. 1

Vilbia: ō Modeste, quam laeta sum! cūr mē ex omnibus puellīs ēlēgistī?

Modestus: necesse est nōbīs in locō sēcrētō noctū convenīre.

Vilbia: id facere nōn ausim. pater mē sōlam exīre nōn vult. ubi est hic locus? 2

Modestus: prope fontem deae Sūlis. nōnne tibi persuādēre possum?

Vilbia: mihi difficile est iussa patris neglegere, sed tibi resistere nōn possum.

Modestus: dā mihi ōsculum. 2

Vilbia: ēheu! ō suspīrium meum! mihi necesse est ad culīnam redīre, tibi noctem exspectāre.

exeunt. Bulbus, quī magnam partem huius colloquiī audīvit, surgit. quam celerrimē ēgressus, Guttam petit, cui cōnsilium callidum prōpōnit.

dīlaniāre *tear to pieces*	sēcrētō: sēcrētus *secret*
ēice: ēicere *throw out*	noctū *by night*
humī *on the ground*	iussa *orders, instructions*
mollīre *soothe*	neglegere *neglect*
clēmentem: clēmēns *merciful*	ēgressus *having gone out*
parcere *spare*	cui *to whom (dative of* quī*)*
victīs: victī *the conquered*	

The sacred spring as it is today

scaena tertia

per silentium noctis thermās intrant Bulbus et Gutta. prope fontem sacrum sē
cēlant. Bulbus Guttae stolam et pallium, quod sēcum tulit, ostendit.

Bulbus: Gutta, volō tē hacc vestīmenta induere. volō tē
persōnam Vilbiae agere. nōbīs necesse est dēcipere
Modestum, quem brevī exspectō.   5

Gutta: vah! virō nōn decōrum est stolam gerere. praetereā
barbam habeō.

Bulbus: id minimī mōmentī est, quod in tenebrīs sumus. nōnne
tibi persuādēre possum? ecce! decem dēnāriōs tibi dō.
nunc tacē! indue stolam palliumque! stā prope fontem 10
deae! ubi Modestus fontī appropinquat, dīc eī verba
suāvissima!

pallium *cloak*	vah! *ugh!*
vestīmenta *clothes*	praetereā *besides*
persōnam Vilbiae agere *play the part of Vilbia*	mōmentī: mōmentum *importance*
brevī *in a short time*	tenebrīs: tenebrae *darkness*

Gutta, postquam stolam invītus induit, prope fontem stat. Modestus, sōlus thermās ingressus, fontī appropinquat.

Modestus: Vilbia, mea Vilbia! Modestus, fortissimus mīlitum, 1! adest.

Gutta: ō dēliciae meae! venī ad mē.

Modestus: quam rauca est vōx tua! num lacrimās, quod tardus adveniō?

Gutta: ita vērō! tam sollicita eram. 2(

Modestus: lacrimās tuās siccāre possum. (*Modestus ad Guttam advenit.*) dī immortālēs! Vilbia! barbam habēs? quid tibi accidit? ō!

tum Bulbus Modestum in fontem dēicit. Vilbia, thermās ingressa, ubi clāmōrēs audīvit, prope iānuam perterrita manet. 2!

Modestus: pereō! pereō! parce! parce!

Bulbus: furcifer! Vilbiam meam, quam valdē amō, auferre audēs? nunc mihi facile est tē interficere.

Modestus: reddō tibi Vilbiam. nōn amō Vilbiam. eam ā tē auferre nōn ausim. nōlī mē innocentem interficere. Vilbiam 30 floccī nōn faciō.

Vilbia, simulatque haec audīvit, īrāta fontī appropinquat. Modestum vituperāre incipit.

Vilbia: mē floccī nōn facis? ō hominem ignāvum! ego ipsa tē dīlaniāre velim. 35

Bulbus: mea Vilbia, victōribus decōrum est victīs parcere.

Vilbia: mī Bulbe, dēliciae meae, miserrima sum! longē errāvī.

Bulbus: nōlī lacrimāre! ego tē cūrāre possum.

Vilbia: ō Bulbe! ō suspīrium meum!

Bulbus et Vilbia domum redeunt. Gutta stolam palliumque exuit. dēnāriōs laetē 40 *numerat. Modestus ē fonte sē extrahit et madidus abit.*

siccāre *dry*
auferre *take away, steal*
longē errāvī: longē errāre *make a big mistake*
exuit: exuere *take off*

About the language

1   Study the following examples:

    homō ingeniī prāvī   a man of evil character
    fēmina magnae dignitātis a woman of great prestige

    In each example, a word like 'homō' or 'fēmina' is described by a noun and adjective in the *genitive* case.

2   Notice the different ways of translating such phrases:

    puella magnae prūdentiae   a girl of great sense
                            or, in more natural English:
                           a very sensible girl

    vir summae virtūtis   a man of the utmost courage
                             or, in more natural English:
                           a very courageous man, *or*
                           a very brave man

3   Further examples:

    vir magnae auctōritātis   fābula huius modī
    homō minimae prūdentiae   iuvenis ingeniī optimī
    vir octōgintā annōrum   puella maximae calliditātis

Practising the language

1 Study the form and meaning of the following adjectives and adverbs, and give the meaning of the untranslated words:

brevis	short	breviter	shortly
ferōx	fierce	ferōciter	fiercely
cōmis	polite	cōmiter	
levis		leviter	lightly, slightly
suāvis	sweet	suāviter	
celer		celeriter	quickly
crūdēlis	cruel	crūdēliter	
mollis	soft, gentle	molliter	
pār		pariter	equally
dīligēns	careful	dīligenter	
neglegēns		neglegenter	carelessly
prūdēns	shrewd, sensible	prūdenter	
audāx	bold	audācter	

Give the meaning of the following adverbs:

fidēliter, fortiter, līberāliter, sapienter, īnsolenter

2 Complete each sentence with the right word and then translate.

1 Modestus per viās ..... ambulābat, puellās quaerēns.
(oppidī, oppidō)

2 Gutta, vir benignus, auxilium ..... saepe dabat. (amīcī,
amīcō)

3 Rubria, quae in tabernā labōrābat, ... vīnum obtulit.
(iuvenis, iuvenī)

4 in vīllā ....., turba ingēns conveniēbat. (haruspicis,
haruspicī)

5 tabernārius ..... multās rēs pretiōsās ostendit. (ancillārum,
ancillīs)

6 dea Sūlis precēs ..... audīre solēbat. (aegrōtōrum, aegrōtīs)

7 centuriō gladiōs hastāsque ..... īnspicere coepit. (mīlitum,
mīlitibus)

8 caupō pessimum vīnum ..... praebēbat. (hospitum,
hospitibus)

3 Make up six Latin sentences using some of the words in the lists below. Some of your sentences should contain four words, but others may contain only three, or two. Write out each sentence and then translate it.

For example: puer senī pōculum trādidit.
The boy handed the cup to the old man.

cīvēs agricolam salūtāvērunt.
The citizens greeted the farmer.

nautās vīdit.
He saw the sailors.

nominatives	accusatives	datives	verbs
servus	pecūniam	ancillīs	vīdit
servī	equōs	fabrō	vīdērunt
gladiātor	dominum	iuvenibus	trādidit
gladiātōrēs	nautās	centuriōnī	trādidērunt
cīvis	leōnem	hominibus	interfēcit
cīvēs	gemmās	senī	interfēcērunt
fēmina	agricolam	spectātōribus	obtulit
fēminae	librōs	medicō	obtulērunt
puer	mīlitem	amīcīs	salūtāvit
puerī	pōculum	rēgī	salūtāvērunt

Magic and curses

When Roman religious sites are excavated, archaeologists sometimes find lead or pewter tablets inscribed with curses. These are known as 'dēfīxiōnēs'. Many Romans believed it was possible to put a curse on a personal enemy by dedicating him or her to the gods in this way.

Many defixiones have been found in Britain. They include, for example, a defixio placed by a man on a gang that had beaten him up. In another one, a woman curses someone who has falsely accused her of poisoning her husband. Many are directed at thieves.

The method of putting a defixio on somebody was as follows. The name of the offender was written on a small tablet together with details of the crime and the hoped-for punishment. The tablet was then fastened to a tomb with a long nail, or thrown into a well or a spring. To increase the mystery the name was often written backwards and apparently meaningless magical words, such as BESCU, BEREBESCU, BAZAGRA, were also added for effect. Sometimes we find a figure roughly drawn on the tablet, as in the illustration opposite. It depicts a bearded demon, carrying an urn and a torch, which were symbols of death. The boat in which he stands may represent the boat of Charon, the ferryman of the Underworld, who took the souls of the dead across the river Styx.

The wording of the curse can be very simple, just 'I dedicate' followed by the intended victim's name. But sometimes it can be ferociously eloquent, as in the following example: 'May burning fever seize all her limbs, kill her soul and her heart. O Gods of the Underworld, break and smash her bones, choke her, let her body be twisted and shattered – phrix, phrox.'

It may seem strange that religion should be used to bring harm to people in this very direct and spiteful way, but the Romans tended to see their gods as possible allies in the struggles of life. When they wished to injure an enemy, they thought it natural and proper to seek the gods' powerful help.

Words and phrases checklist

adeptus, adepta, adeptum – having received, having obtained
amor, amōris – love
aureus, aurea, aureum – golden, made of gold
avidē – eagerly
caelum, caelī – sky
dēcipiō, dēcipere, dēcēpī, dēceptus – deceive, trick
dīrus, dīra, dīrum – dreadful
dissentiō, dissentīre, dissēnsī – disagree
ēligō, ēligere, ēlēgī, ēlēctus – choose
exitium, exitiī – ruin, destruction
fundō, fundere, fūdī, fūsus – pour
hostis, hostis – enemy
iactō, iactāre, iactāvī, iactātus – throw
incipiō, incipere, incēpī, inceptus – begin
ingressus, ingressa, ingressum – having entered
iniciō, inicere, iniēcī, iniectus – throw in
lacrima, lacrimae – tear
minimus, minima, minimum – very little, least
molestus, molesta, molestum – troublesome
moneō, monēre, monuī, monitus – warn, advise
parcō, parcere, pepercī – spare
precātus, precāta, precātum – having prayed (to)
prūdentia, prūdentiae – prudence, good sense
quantus, quanta, quantum – how big
quō modō? – how?
tardus, tarda, tardum – late
tūtus, tūta, tūtum – safe
verbum, verbī – word
virtūs, virtūtis – courage
vītō, vītāre, vītāvī, vītātus – avoid

haruspex

in thermīs

I

prope thermās erat templum, ā fabrīs Cogidubnī aedificātum. in
hōc templō aegrōtī deam Sūlem adōrāre solēbant. rēx Cogidubnus
cum multīs prīncipibus servīsque prō templō sedēbat. Quīntus
prope sellam rēgis stābat. rēgem prīncipēsque manus mīlitum
custōdiēbat. prō templō erat āra ingēns, quam omnēs aspiciēbant. 5
Memor, togam praetextam gerēns, prope āram stābat.

duo sacerdōtēs, agnam nigram dūcentēs, ad āram prōcessērunt.
postquam rēx signum dedit, ūnus sacerdōs agnam sacrificāvit.
deinde Memor, quī iam tremēbat sūdābatque, alterī sacerdōtī dīxit,
'iubeō tē ōmina īnspicere. dīc mihi: quid vidēs?' 10
sacerdōs, postquam iecur agnae īnspexit, anxius,
'iecur est līvidum', inquit. 'nōnne hoc mortem significat? nōnne
mortem virī clārī significat?'

Memor, quī perterritus pallēscēbat, sacerdōtī respondit,
'minimē! dea Sūlis, quae precēs aegrōtōrum audīre solet, nōbīs 15
ōmina optima mīsit.'

haec verba locūtus, ad Cogidubnum sē vertit et clāmāvit,
'ōmina sunt optima! ōmina tibi remedium mīrābile significant,
quod dea Sūlis Minerva tibi favet.'

tum rēgem ac prīncipēs Memor in apodytērium dūxit. 20

manus mīlitum *a band of soldiers*
aspiciēbant: aspicere *look towards*
praetextam: praetextus *with a purple border*
agnam: agna *lamb*
ōmina *omens (signs from the gods)*
iecur *liver*
līvidum: līvidus *lead-coloured*
significat: significāre *mean, indicate*
pallēscēbat: pallēscere *grow pale*
ac *and*

II

deinde omnēs in eam partem thermārum intrāvērunt, ubi balneum
maximum erat. Quīntus, prīncipēs secūtus, circumspectāvit et
attonitus dīxit,
    'hae thermae maiōrēs sunt quam thermae Pompēiānae!'
    servī cum magnā difficultāte Cogidubnum in balneum dēmittere 5
coepērunt. maximus clāmor erat. rēx prīncipibus mandāta dabat.
prīncipēs lībertōs suōs vituperābant, lībertī servōs.
    tandem rēx, ē balneō ēgressus, vestīmenta, quae servī tulerant,
induit. tum omnēs fontī sacrō appropinquāvērunt.
    'ubi est pōculum?' rogāvit Cogidubnus. 'nōbīs decōrum est 10
aquam sacram bibere. aqua est amāra, sed remedium potentis-
simum.'

secūtus *having followed*
difficultāte: difficultās *difficulty*
dēmittere *let down, lower*
amāra: amārus *bitter*

haec verba locūtus, rēx ad fontem sacrum prōcessit. Cephalus, quī anxius tremēbat, prope fontem stābat, pōculum ōrnātissimum tenēns. rēgī pōculum obtulit. rēx pōculum ad labra sustulit. subitō 1 Quīntus, pōculum cōnspicātus, manum rēgis prēnsāvit et clāmāvit, 'nōlī bibere! hoc est pōculum venēnātum. pōculum huius modī in urbe Alexandrīā vīdī.'

'longē errās', respondit rēx. 'nēmō mihi nocēre vult. nēmō umquam mortem mihi parāre temptāvit.' 2

'rēx summae virtūtis es', respondit Quīntus. 'sed, quamquam nūllum perīculum timēs, tūtius est tibi vērum scīre. pōculum īnspicere velim. dā mihi!'

tum pōculum Quīntus īnspicere coepit. Cephalus tamen pōculum ē manibus Quīntī rapere temptābat. maxima pars 2 spectātōrum stābat immōta. sed Dumnorix, prīnceps Rēgnēnsium, saeviēbat tamquam leō furēns. pōculum rapuit et Cephalō obtulit.

'facile est nōbīs vērum cognōscere', clāmāvit. 'iubeō tē pōculum haurīre. num aquam bibere timēs?'

Cephalus pōculum haurīre nōluit, et ad genua rēgis prōcubuit. 3 rēx immōtus stābat. cēterī prīncipēs lībertum frūstrā resistentem prēnsāvērunt. Cephalus, ā prīncipibus coāctus, venēnum hausit. deinde, vehementer tremēns, gemitum ingentem dedit et mortuus prōcubuit.

labra *lips*
prēnsāvit: prēnsāre *take hold of, clutch*
genua *knees*
coāctus: cōgere *force, compel*

epistula Cephalī

postquam Cephalus periit, servus eius rēgī epistulam trādidit, ā Cephalō ipsō scrīptam:

'rēx Cogidubne, in maximō perīculō es. Memor īnsānit. mortem tuam cupit. iussit mē rem efficere. invītus Memorī pāruī. fortasse mihi nōn crēdis. sed tōtam rem tibi nārrāre velim. 5

ubi tū ad hās thermās advēnistī, remedium quaerēns, Memor mē ad vīllam suam arcessīvit. vīllam ingressus, Memorem perterritum invēnī. attonitus eram. numquam Memorem adeō perterritum vīderam. Memor mihi,

"Imperātor mortem Cogidubnī cupit", inquit. "iubeō tē hanc 10 rem administrāre. iubeō tē venēnum parāre. tibi necesse est eum interficere. Cogidubnus enim est homō ingeniī prāvī."

Memorī respondī,

"longē errās. Cogidubnus est vir ingeniī optimī. tālem rem facere nōlō." 15

Memor īrātus mihi respondit,

"sceleste! lībertus meus es, et servus meus crās. tē līberāvī et multam pecuniam dedī. mandāta mea facere dēbēs. cūr mihi obstās?"

rēx Cogidubne, diū recūsāvī obstinātus. diū beneficia tua 20 commemorāvī. tandem Memor custōdem arcessīvit, quī mē verberāvit. ā custōde paene interfectus, Memorī tandem cessī.

ad casam meam regressus, venēnum invītus parāvī. scrīpsī tamen hanc epistulam et servō fidēlī trādidī. iussī servum tibi epistulam trādere. veniam petō, quamquam facinus scelestum parāvī. Memor 25 nocēns est. Memor coēgit mē hanc rem efficere. Memorem, nōn mē, pūnīre dēbēs.'

īnsānit: īnsānīre *be mad, be insane*
beneficia *acts of kindness, favours*
facinus *crime*
coēgit: cōgere *force, compel*

About the language

1   You have now met the plural of neuter nouns like 'templum' and
'nōmen':

sunt multa **templa** in hāc urbe.
There are many temples in this city.

lībertus **nōmina** prīncipum recitāvit.
The freedman read out the names of the chieftains.

2   Study the nominative and accusative forms of the following
neuter nouns:

	singular		*plural*	
	nominative	*accusative*	*nominative*	*accusative*
2nd declension	templum	templum	templa	templa
	aedificium	aedificium	aedificia	aedificia
3rd declension	nōmen	nōmen	nōmina	nōmina
	caput	caput	capita	capita
	mare	mare	maria	maria

3   Further examples:

1 aedificium erat splendidissimum.
2 ubi haec verba audīvit, Memor tacēbat.
3 fēlēs caput hominis rāsit.
4 Cephalus cōnsilium subitō cēpit.
5 haec cubicula sunt sordidissima.
6 servī pōcula ad prīncipēs tulērunt.

When you have read this, answer the questions at the end.

Britannia perdomita

Salvius cum Memore anxius colloquium habet. servus ingressus ad Memorem currit.

servus: domine, rēx Cogidubnus hūc venit. rēx togam praetextam ōrnāmentaque gerit. magnum numerum mīlitum secum dūcit.   5

Memor: rēx mīlitēs hūc dūcit? togam praetextam gerit?

Salvius: Cogidubnus, nōs suspicātus, ultiōnem petit. Memor, tibi necesse est mē adiuvāre. nōs enim Rōmānī sumus, Cogidubnus barbarus.

             (*intrat Cogidubnus. in manibus epistulam tenet, ā Cephalō* 10
             scrīptam.)

Cogidubnus: Memor, tū illās īnsidiās parāvistī. tū iussistī Cephalum venēnum comparāre et mē necāre. sed Cephalus, lībertus tuus, mihi omnia patefēcit.

Memor: Cogidubne, id quod dīcis, absurdum est. mortuus est 15 Cephalus.

perdomita: perdomitus *conquered*
suspicātus *having suspected*
ultiōnem: ultiō *revenge*
patefēcit: patefacere *reveal*
absurdum: absurdus *absurd*

DE BRITANNIS

Cogidubnus: Cephalus homō magnae prūdentiae erat. tibi nōn crēdidit. invītus tibi pāruit. simulac mandāta ista dedistī, scrīpsit Cephalus epistulam in quā omnia patefēcit. servus, ā Cephalō missus, epistulam mihi 20 tulit.

Memor: epistula falsa est, servus mendācissimus.

Cogidubnus: tū, nōn servus, es mendāx. servus enim, multa tormenta passus, in eādem sententiā mānsit.

Salvius: Cogidubne, cūr mīlitēs hūc dūxistī? 25

Cogidubnus: Memorem ē cūrā thermārum iam dēmōvī.

Memor: quid dīcis? tū mē dēmōvistī? innocēns sum. Salv- . . .

Salvius: rēx Cogidubne, quid fēcistī? tū, quī barbarus es, haruspicem Rōmānum dēmovēre audēs? nimium audēs! tū, summōs honōrēs ā nōbīs adeptus, 30 numquam contentus fuistī. nōs diū vexāvistī. nunc dēnique, cum mīlitibus hūc ingressus, perfidiam apertē ostendis. Imperātor Domitiānus, arrogantiam tuam diū passus, ad mē epistulam nūper mīsit. in hāc epistulā iussit mē rēgnum tuum occupāre. iubeō tē 35 igitur ad aulam statim redīre.

Cogidubnus: ēn iūstitia Rōmāna! ēn fidēs! nūllī perfidiōrēs sunt quam Rōmānī. stultissimus fuī, quod Rōmānīs adhūc crēdidī. amīcōs meōs prōdidī; rēgnum meum āmīsī. ōlim, ā Rōmānīs dēceptus, ōrnāmenta honōrēsque 40 Rōmānōs accēpī. hodiē ista ōrnāmenta, mihi ā Rōmānīs data, humī iaciō. Salvī, mitte nūntium ad istum Imperātōrem, 'nōs Cogidubnum tandem vīcimus. Britannia perdomita est.'

(*senex, haec locūtus, lentē per iānuam exit.*) 45

falsa: falsus *false, untrue*	rēgnum *kingdom*
tormenta *torture*	occupāre *seize, take over*
passus *having suffered*	ēn iūstitia! *so this is justice!*
eādem *the same*	fidēs *loyalty, trustworthiness*
dēmōvī: dēmovēre *dismiss*	perfidiōrēs: perfidus *treacherous, untrustworthy*
perfidiam: perfidia *treachery*	adhūc *up till now*
apertē *openly*	prōdidī: prōdere *betray*
	vīcimus: vincere *conquer*

1 When Memor and Salvius hear of Cogidubnus' arrival, do they think this is an ordinary visit, or a special one? What makes them think so?
2 What reason does Salvius give for saying that Memor ought to support him against Cogidubnus?
3 How has Cogidubnus found out about the poison plot?
4 What action has Cogidubnus taken against Memor? Was this action wise or foolish?
5 Which word in line 29 is used by Salvius to contrast with 'barbarus' in line 28?
6 What orders does Salvius say he has recently received? From whom?
7 Why does Cogidubnus fling his 'ōrnāmenta' to the ground?

Practising the language

1 Study the form and meaning of the following verbs and nouns, and give the meaning of the untranslated words. The verb is given in its infinitive form; sometimes the perfect passive participle has been added in brackets.

arāre	to plough	arātor	ploughman
pingere (pictus)	to paint	pictor	painter
vincere (victus)	to win	victor	
emere (ēmptus)		ēmptor	buyer, purchaser
praecurrere	to run ahead	praecursor	
dūcere (ductus)	to lead	ductor	
legere (lēctus)		lēctor	reader
gubernāre	to steer	gubernātor	
amāre	to love	amātor	
spectāre		spectātor	
favēre		fautor	
		(*written in early Latin as* 'favitor')	

Give the meaning of the following nouns:

dēfēnsor, oppugnātor, vēnditor, saltātor, prōditor

2 Complete each sentence with the right word and then translate.

1 nōs ancillae fessae sumus; semper in vīllā . . . . . .
(labōrāmus, labōrātis, labōrant)

2 'quid faciunt illī servī?' 'saxa ad plaustrum . . . . . .' (ferimus,
fertis, ferunt)

3 fīlius meus vōbīs grātiās agere vult, quod mē . . . . . .
(servāvimus, servāvistis, servāvērunt)

4 quamquam prope āram . . . . ., sacrificium vidēre nōn
poterāmus. (stābāmus, stābātis, stābant)

5 ubi prīncipēs fontī . . . . ., Cephalus prōcessit, pōculum
tenēns. (appropinquābāmus, appropinquābātis, appropinquābant)

6 in maximō perīculō estis, quod fīlium rēgis . . . . . .
(interfēcimus, interfēcistis, interfēcērunt)

7 nōs, quī fontem sacrum numquam . . . . ., ad thermās cum
rēge īre cupiēbāmus. (vīderāmus, vīderātis, vīderant)

8 dominī nostrī sunt benignī; nōbīs semper satis cibī . . . . . .
(praebēmus, praebētis, praebent)

3 Translate the verbs in the left-hand column then, keeping the
person and number unchanged, use the verb in brackets to form
a phrase with the infinitive and translate again. For example:

respondēmus.   (volō)   This becomes: respondēre volumus.
We reply.   We want to reply.
festīnat.   (dēbeō)   This becomes: festīnāre dēbet.
He hurries.   He ought to hurry.

The present tense of 'volō' and 'possum' is set out on page 174 in
the Language Information section; 'dēbeō' is a second
conjugation verb like 'doceō' (see Language Information
section, p.170).

1 dormītis.   (dēbeō)
2 sedēmus.   (volō)
3 pugnat.   (possum)
4 labōrant.   (dēbeō)
5 revenīmus.   (possum)
6 num nāvigās? (volō)

4 Complete each sentence with the most suitable participle from the list below and then translate.

locūtus, ingressus, missus, excitātus, superātus

1 Cogidubnus, haec verba . . . . ., ab aulā discessit.
2 nūntius, ab amīcīs meīs . . . . ., epistulam mihi trādidit.
3 fūr, vīllam . . . . ., cautē circumspectāvit.
4 Bulbus, ā Modestō . . . . ., sub mēnsā iacēbat.
5 haruspex, ā Cephalō . . . . ., invītus ē lectō surrēxit.

Roman religion

The stories in Stages 22 and 23 have mentioned two ways in which religion played a part in Roman life. In Stage 22, Bulbus sought the help of the gods against his enemy Modestus by means of a defixio; in Stage 23, Memor has been carrying out his duties as a 'haruspex' or soothsayer, by supervising a sacrifice and ordering the examination of the victim's internal organs (entrails). This was one of the ways in which the Romans tried to foretell the future and discover what the gods had in store for them. An invalid hoping for a cure, a general about to fight a battle, and a merchant just before a long business journey, might all consult a haruspex to try to discover their chances of success.

An animal would be sacrificed to the appropriate god or goddess; it was hoped that this would please the god and encourage him to look favourably on the sacrificer. The haruspex and his assistants would make careful observations. They would watch the way in which the victim fell; they would observe the smoke and flames when parts of the victim were placed on the altar fire; and, above all, they would cut the victim open and examine its entrails, especially the liver. They would look for anything unusual about the liver's size or shape, observe its colour and texture and note whether it had spots on its surface. They would then interpret what they saw and announce to the sacrificer whether the signs from the gods were favourable or not.

Bronze liver marked with the different areas to be observed by the haruspex

Such attempts to discover the future were known as divination. Another type of divination was performed by priests known as augurs who based their predictions on observations of the flight of birds. They would note the direction of flight, and observe whether the birds flew together or separately, what kind of birds they were and what noises they made.

Roman religion involved many other beliefs, habits and ceremonies, and it developed over many centuries. The early Romans, in common with many primitive peoples, believed that all things were controlled by spirits which they called 'nūmina'. They had looked at fire and been terrified by its power to burn and destroy, yet excited by its power to cook, warm and provide light. They had seen the regular sequence of day and night and of the seasons of the year but were unable to explain their causes scientifically. Not surprisingly, therefore, they believed that the power of numina was at work, and they soon realised it was important to ensure that the numina used their power for good rather than harm. For this reason the early Romans presented them with offerings of food and wine. At special times of the year, such as seed-time or harvest, an animal would be slaughtered and offered as a sacrifice to the numina. In this way ceremonies and rituals developed at fixed points in the year and gradually communities began to construct calendars to record them.

When the Romans came into contact with the peoples of the Greek world, they began to realise that their own vague and shapeless spirits were imagined by the Greeks as all-powerful gods and goddesses who had not only names and physical shapes but also human characteristics. The Roman corn-spirit, Ceres, became identified with the Greek goddess, Demeter, mother of all life-giving nourishment. The Greeks told stories (myths) about their gods and goddesses which helped to explain more vividly the workings of the world. For example, they said that Demeter's daughter, Persephone, had been carried off by her wicked uncle, Dis, ruler of the Underworld, and was only allowed to return to the earth for six months of the year. In this way a myth was used to explain the rebirth of nature each spring: as Persephone returned each year, Demeter stopped grieving and allowed life back to the countryside.

The Romans were also in contact with the Etruscans, a powerful race who lived in central Italy to the north of Rome. From them they borrowed the practice of divination, described above.

The worship of the gods and goddesses and the practice of divination became central features of the Roman state religion. The rituals and ceremonies were organised by colleges of priests and other religious officials, and the festivals and sacrifices were carried out by them on behalf of the state. The emperor always held the position of 'Pontifex Maximus' or Chief Priest. Great attention was paid to the details of worship. Every word had to be pronounced correctly, otherwise the whole ceremony had to be restarted; a pipe-player was employed to drown noises and cries which were thought to be unlucky for the ritual. Everyone who watched the ceremonies had to stand quite still and silent, like Plancus in the Stage 17 story.

In addition to these public ceremonies, many citizens kept up the practice of private family worship. This included offerings to Vesta, the spirit of the hearth, and to the lares and penates, the spirits of the household and store-cupboard. Such practices were probably more common in the country districts than they were in Rome itself. The head of the household (paterfamiliās) was responsible for performing the rituals and chanting the prayers. Even here everything had to be done correctly and many Roman prayers are worded to make sure that no god or goddess was forgotten or missed out by mistake. It was important to address the god or goddess by the right name, as in this example from a poem by Catullus:

> You are called Juno Lucina
> by women in childbirth,
> you are called nightly Trivia, and Luna
> whose light is not your own.
> . . . may you be hallowed
> by whatever name pleases you . . .

Catullus was, in fact, addressing the goddess Diana, but he used some of her other names to make sure she would attend to his prayer.

The Romans tended to regard prayer as a means of asking for favours from the gods and accompanied their prayers with promises of offerings if the favours were granted. These promises were known as 'vōta'. It would not be an exaggeration to say that many Romans saw religion as a kind of 'business deal' with the gods. A common phrase in prayers was: 'dō ut dēs' – 'I give so that you may give'.

When the Romans arrived in Britain, they found that the Celtic religion was very similar to their own earlier belief in numina. Under Roman influence, the Celts began to identify their spirits with the Roman gods and goddesses, just as the Romans had adopted the Greek gods and goddesses several centuries earlier. The following inscription is a good example of this: 'Peregrinus, son of Secundus, a Treveran, to Mars Loucetius and Nemetona willingly and with good cause fulfilled his vow.' The Roman god Mars and the Celtic god Loucetius are presented here as one god with one name, just as Sulis and Minerva had merged into one goddess at Aquae Sulis. The Romans made no attempt to convert the Celts to a belief in Roman religion. However, they knew that by identifying Roman gods with Celtic ones, they would encourage the British to accept Roman rule more readily.

Another feature of Roman religion which was intended to

Head of the goddess Minerva

encourage acceptance of Roman rule was the worship of the emperor. In Rome itself, emperor worship was officially discouraged. However, the peoples of the eastern provinces of the Roman empire had always regarded their kings and rulers as divine and were equally ready to pay divine honours to the Roman emperors. Gradually the Romans introduced this idea in the west as well. The Britons and other western peoples were encouraged to worship the 'genius' (protecting spirit) of the emperor, linked with the goddess Roma. Altars were erected in honour of 'Rome and the emperor'. When an emperor died it was usual to deify him (make him a god), and temples were often built to honour the deified emperor in the provinces. One such temple, that of Claudius in Colchester, was destroyed by the British before it was even finished, during the revolt led by Queen Boudica in A.D. 60. The historian

Tacitus tells us why:

'The temple dedicated to the deified Emperor Claudius seemed to the British a symbol of everlasting oppression, and the chosen priests used religion as an excuse for wasting British money.'

Clearly the British found it hard to accept the idea of emperor worship at first.

Words and phrases checklist

administrō, administrāre, administrāvī – look after, manage

cēdō, cēdere, cessī – give in, give way

clārus, clāra, clārum – famous

commemorō, commemorāre, commemorāvī, commemorātus – mention, recall

cōnspicātus, cōnspicāta, cōnspicātum – having caught sight of

cūra, cūrae – care

enim – for

errō, errāre, errāvī – make a mistake

gerō, gerere, gessī, gestus – wear

honor, honōris – honour

iaciō, iacere, iēcī, iactus – throw

immōtus, immōta, immōtum – still, motionless

induō, induere, induī, indūtus – put on

ingenium, ingeniī – character

locūtus, locūta, locūtum – having spoken

mandātum, mandātī – instruction, order

modus, modī – manner, way, kind

rēs huius modī – a thing of this kind

nimium – too much

numerus, numerī – number

ōrnō, ōrnāre, ōrnāvī, ōrnātus – decorate

pāreō, pārēre, pāruī – obey

potēns, *gen.* potentis – powerful

prāvus, prāva, prāvum – evil

regressus, regressa, regressum – having returned

scio, scīre, scīvī – know

tālis, tāle – such

tamquam – as, like

umquam – ever

venēnum, venēnī – poison

venia, veniae – mercy

fuga

in itinere

Modestus et Strȳthiō, ex oppidō Aquīs Sūlis ēgressī, Dēvam
equitābant. in itinere ad flūmen altum vēnērunt, ubi erat pōns
sēmirutus. cum ad pontem vēnissent, equus trānsīre nōluit.

'equus trānsīre timet', inquit Modestus. 'Strȳthiō, tū prīmus
trānsī!'   5

cum Strȳthiō trānsiisset, equus trānsīre etiam tum nōlēbat.
Modestus igitur ex equō dēscendit. cum dēscendisset, equus statim
trānsiit.

'eque! redī!' inquit Modestus. 'mē dēseruistī.'

equus tamen in alterā rīpā immōtus stetit. Modestus cautissimē 10
trānsīre coepit. cum ad medium pontem vēnisset, dēcidit pōns,
dēcidit Modestus. mediīs ex undīs clāmāvit,

'caudicēs, vōs pontem labefēcistis.'

Dēvam *to Chester*   sēmirutus *rickety*
altum: altus *deep*   labefēcistis: labefacere *weaken*

When you have read this story, answer the questions at the end.

Quīntus cōnsilium capit

cum Cogidubnus trīstis īrātusque ē vīllā Memoris exiisset, Salvius
mīlitēs quīnquāgintā arcessīvit. eōs iussit rēgem prīncipēsque
Rēgnēnsium comprehendere et in carcere retinēre. hī mīlitēs, tōtum
per oppidum missī, mox rēgem cum prīncipibus invēnērunt. eōs
statim comprehendērunt. Dumnorix tamen, ē manibus mīlitum 5
ēlāpsus, per viās oppidī noctū prōcessit et Quīntum quaesīvit.
Quīntō enim crēdēbat.

cubiculum Quīntī ingressus, haec dīxit:

'amīce, tibi crēdere possum. adiuvā mē, adiuvā Cogidubnum.
paucīs Rōmānīs crēdō; plūrimī sunt perfidī. nēmō quidem perfidior 1
est quam iste Salvius quī Cogidubnum interficere nūper temptāvit.
nunc Cogidubnus, ā mīlitibus Salviī comprehēnsus, in carcere iacet.
Salvius crīmen maiestātis in eum īnferre cupit. rēx, in carcere
inclūsus, omnīnō dē vītā suā dēspērat.

'tū tamen es vir summae virtūtis magnaeque prūdentiae. 1
quamquam Salvius potentissimus et īnfestissimus est, nōlī rēgem
dēserere. nōlī eum, ab homine scelestō oppugnātum, relinquere. tū
anteā eum servāvistī. nōnne iterum servāre potes?'

cum Dumnorix haec dīxisset, Quīntus rem sēcum anxius
cōgitābat. auxilium Cogidubnō ferre volēbat, quod eum valdē 2
dīligēbat; sed rēs difficillima erat. subitō cōnsilium cēpit.

'nōlī dēspērāre!' exclāmāvit. 'rēgī auxilium ferre possumus. hanc
rem ad lēgātum Gnaeum Iūlium Agricolam clam referre dēbēmus.
itaque nōbīs festīnandum est ad ultimās partēs Britanniae ubi
Agricola bellum gerit. eī vēra patefacere possumus. Agricola sōlus 2
Salviō obstāre potest, quod summam potestātem in Britanniā
habet. nunc nōbīs hinc effugiendum est.'

Dumnorix, cum haec audīvisset, cōnsilium audāx magnopere
laudāvit. tum Quīntus servum fīdissimum arcessīvit, cui mandāta
dedit. servus exiit. mox regressus, cibum sex diērum Quīntō et 3

Dumnorigī trādidit. illī, ē vīllā ēlāpsī, per viās dēsertās cautē prōcessērunt.

vīllam Memoris praetereuntēs, Quīntus et Dumnorix duōs equōs cōnspexērunt, ad pālum dēligātōs. Quīntus, quī fūrtum committere nōlēbat, haesitāvit. 35

Dumnorix rīdēns 'nōlī haesitāre', inquit. 'hī sunt equī Salviī.'

Quīntus et Dumnorix equōs cōnscendērunt et ad ultimās partēs īnsulae abiērunt.

carcere: carcer *prison*
ēlāpsus *having escaped*
quidem *indeed*
crīmen maiestātis *charge of treason*
īnferre *bring against*
inclūsus *shut up, imprisoned*
omnīnō *completely*
sēcum . . . cōgitābat *considered*
    . . . *to himself*
dīligēbat: dīligere *be fond of*
nōbīs festīnandum est *we must hurry*
ultimās: ultimus *furthest*
bellum gerit: bellum gerere *wage war, campaign*

potestātem: potestās *power*
magnopere *greatly*
fīdissimum: fīdus *trustworthy*
diērum: diēs *day*
praetereuntēs: praeterīre *pass by, go past*
pālum: pālus *stake, post*
fūrtum *theft, robbery*
committere *commit*
haesitāvit: haesitāre *hesitate*
cōnscendērunt: cōnscendere *mount, climb on*

1 How many soldiers does Salvius send for? What does he tell them to do?
2 Which British chieftain escapes? Whose help does he seek, and why?
3 What further action does Salvius intend to take against Cogidubnus?
4 What events is Dumnorix referring to when he says 'tū anteā eum servāvistī' (lines 17–18)?
5 What does Quintus suggest? Why does he think Agricola can stop Salvius?
6 How many days' food do Quintus and Dumnorix take with them? How do they obtain horses?
7 Why does Quintus support a British king and a British chieftain, instead of supporting his fellow-Roman Salvius?

About the language

1 Study the following sentences:

cum Modestus ad pontem **advēnisset**, equus cōnstitit.
When Modestus had arrived at the bridge, the horse stopped.

cum coquus omnia **parāvisset**, mercātor amīcōs in triclīnium
dūxit.
When the cook had got everything ready, the merchant led his
friends into the dining-room.

The form of the verb in heavy print is known as the *subjunctive*.

2 The subjunctive is often used with the word 'cum' meaning
'when', as in the examples above.

3 Further examples:

1 cum rēx exiisset, Salvius mīlitēs ad sē vocāvit.
2 cum gladiātōrēs leōnem interfēcissent, spectātōrēs
plausērunt.
3 cum dominus haec mandāta dedisset, fabrī ad aulam
rediērunt.
4 fūrēs, cum cubiculum intrāvissent, tacitī circumspectāv-
ērunt.

4 The examples of the subjunctive in paragraphs 1 and 3 are all in
the same tense: the *pluperfect subjunctive*. Compare the pluperfect
subjunctive with the ordinary form of the pluperfect:

pluperfect	*pluperfect subjunctive*	
3rd person singular	*3rd person singular*	*3rd person plural*
trāxerat	trāxisset	trāxissent
ambulāverat	ambulāvisset	ambulāvissent
dormīverat	dormīvisset	dormīvissent
voluerat	voluisset	voluissent
fuerat	fuisset	fuissent

Salvius cōnsilium cognōscit

postrīdiē mīlitēs Dumnorigem per oppidum quaerēbant. cum eum
nusquam invenīre potuissent, rem dēnique Salviō nūntiāvērunt.
ille, cum dē fugā Dumnorigis cognōvisset, vehementer saeviēbat;
omnēs mīlitēs, quī Dumnorigem custōdīverant, poenās dare iussit.
Quīntum quoque quaesīvit; invenīre tamen nōn poterat. tum 5
Belimicum, prīncipem Canticōrum, arcessīvit.

    'Belimice', inquit, 'iste Dumnorix ē manibus meīs effūgit; abest
quoque Quīntus Caecilius. neque Dumnorigī neque Quīntō crēdō.
Quīntus enim saepe Dumnorigī favēbat, saepe cum eō colloquium
habēbat. ī nunc; dūc mīlitēs tēcum; illōs quaere in omnibus partibus 10

nusquam *nowhere*   fugā: fuga *escape*   ī: īre *go*

oppidī. quaere servōs quoque eōrum. facile est nōbīs servōs torquēre et vērum ita cognōscere.'

Belimicus, multīs cum mīlitibus ēgressus, per oppidum dīligenter quaerēbat. intereā Salvius anxius reditum eius exspectābat. cum Salvius rem sēcum cōgitāret, Belimicus subitō rediit exsultāns. servum Quīntī in medium ātrium trāxit.

'fūgērunt illī scelestī', clāmāvit, 'sed hic servus, captus et interrogatus, vērum patefēcit.'

Salvius ad servum trementem conversus,

'ubi est Quīntus Caecilius?' inquit. 'quō fūgit Dumnorix?'

'nescio', inquit servus quī, multa tormenta passus, iam vix quicquam dīcere poterat. 'nihil scio', iterum inquit.

Belimicus, cum haec audīvisset, gladium dēstrictum ad iugulum servī tenuit.

'melius est tibi', inquit, 'vērum Salviō dīcere.'

servus quī iam dē vītā suā dēspērābat,

'cibum sex diērum tantum parāvī', inquit susurrāns. 'nihil aliud fēcī. dominus meus cum Dumnorige in ultimās partēs Britanniae discessit.'

Salvius 'hercle!' inquit. 'ad Agricolam iērunt. Quīntus, ā Dumnorige incitātus, mihi obstāre temptat; homō tamen magnae stultitiae est; mihi resistere nōn potest, quod ego maiōrem auctōritātem habeō quam ille.'

Salvius, cum haec dīxisset, Belimicō mandāta dedit. eum iussit cum ducentīs equitibus exīre et fugitīvōs comprehendere. servum carnificibus trādidit. deinde scrībam arcessīvit cui epistulam dictāvit. ūnum ē servīs suīs iussit hanc epistulam quam celerrimē ad Agricolam ferre.

intereā Belimicus, Quīntum et Dumnorigem per multōs diēs secūtus, eōs tandem invēnit. equitēs statim impetum in eōs fēcērunt. amīcī, ab equitibus circumventī, fortiter resistēbant. dēnique Dumnorix humī cecidit mortuus; Quīntus vulnerātus magnā cum difficultāte effūgit.

torquēre *torture*	quicquam *anything*
reditum: reditus *return*	dēstrictum: dēstringere *draw*
exsultāns: exsultāre *exult, be triumphant*	iugulum *throat*
conversus *having turned*	fugitīvōs: fugitīvus *fugitive*
	scrībam: scrība *secretary*

About the language

1   At the beginning of this Stage, you met sentences with 'cum' and the *pluperfect subjunctive*:

senex, cum pecūniam **invēnisset**, ad vīllam laetus rediit.
When the old man had found the money, he returned happily to the villa.

cum rem **cōnfēcissent**, abiērunt.
When they had finished the job, they went away.

2   Now study the following examples:

cum custōdēs **dormīrent**, captīvī ē carcere effūgērunt.
When the guards were sleeping, the prisoners escaped from the prison.

Modestus, cum in Britanniā **mīlitāret**, multās puellās amābat.
When Modestus was serving in the army in Britain, he loved many girls.

In these sentences, 'cum' is being used with a different tense of the subjunctive: the *imperfect subjunctive*.

3   Further examples:

1 cum hospitēs cēnam cōnsūmerent, fūr cubiculum intrāvit.
2 cum prīnceps rem cōgitāret, nūntiī subitō revēnērunt.
3 iuvenēs, cum bēstiās agitārent, mīlitem vulnerātum cōnspexērunt.
4 puella, cum epistulam scrīberet, sonitum mīrābilem audīvit.

4   Compare the imperfect subjunctive with the infinitive:

infinitive	*imperfect subjunctive*	
	3rd person singular	*3rd person plural*
trahere	traheret	traherent
ambulāre	ambulāret	ambulārent
dormīre	dormīret	dormīrent
velle	vellet	vellent
esse	esset	essent

Practising the language

1 Study the form and meaning of the following, and give the
meaning of the untranslated words:

volō	I want	nōlō	I do not want
scīre	to know	nescīre	not to know
umquam	ever	numquam	
usquam	anywhere	nusquam	
fās	right, lawful	nefās	

patiēns		impatiēns	impatient
mortālis		immortālis	
sānus	of sound mind	īnsānus	
memor	remembering	immemor	
fēlīx		īnfēlīx	unlucky
amīcus	friend	inimīcus	
ūtilis		inūtilis	useless
pavidus		impavidus	fearless
nōtus	known, well-known	ignōtus	
aequus	fair, equal	inīquus	

cōnsentīre	to agree	dissentīre	
facilis		difficilis	difficult
similis		dissimilis	unlike

Notice again the meanings of three pairs of words which you
have already met:

ōtium	leisure	neg-ōtium	non-leisure, i.e. business
legere	to read, to attend to	neg-legere	not to attend to, i.e. to neglect
homō	man	nēmō	no man, i.e. nobody

Give the meaning of the following words:

immōtus, incertus, incrēdibilis, indignus, ingrātus, nocēns

2 With the help of paragraph 5 on page 167 in the Language Information section, replace the words in heavy print with the correct form of the pronoun 'is' and then translate. For example:

Rūfilla in hortō ambulābat. Quīntus **Rūfillam** salūtāvit.
This becomes:
Rūfilla in hortō ambulābat. Quīntus eam salūtāvit.
Rufilla was walking in the garden. Quintus greeted her.

In sentences 7 and 8, you may need to look up the gender of a noun in the 'Words and phrases' part of the Language Information section.

1 Quīntus mox ad aulam advēnit. ancilla **Quīntum** in ātrium dūxit.
2 Salvius in lectō recumbēbat. puer **Salviō** plūs cibī obtulit.
3 Rūfilla laetissima erat; marītus **Rūfillae** tamen nōn erat contentus.
4 Britannī ferōciter pugnāvērunt, sed legiōnēs nostrae tandem **Britannōs** vīcērunt.
5 barbarī impetum in nōs fēcērunt. **barbarīs** autem restitimus.
6 multae fēminae prō templō conveniēbant. līberī **fēminārum** quoque aderant.
7 in illō oppidō est fōns sacer; **fontem** saepe vīsitāvī.
8 in Britanniā sunt trēs legiōnēs; imperātor **legiōnēs** iussit barbaros vincere.

3 Complete each sentence with the right word and then translate.

1 subitō ancilla . . . . . in ātrium irrūpit. (perterrita, perterritae)
2 rēx, postquam hoc audīvit, fabrōs . . . . . dīmīsit. (fessum, fessōs)
3 centuriō quī adstābat custōdēs . . . . . laudāvit. (callidum, callidōs)
4 omnēs cīvēs nāvem . . . . . spectābant. (sacram, sacrās)
5 ubi in magnō perīculō eram, amīcus . . . . . mē servāvit. (fidēlis, fidēlēs)
6 'in illā īnsulā', inquit senex, 'habitant multī virī . . . . . .' (ferōx, ferōcēs)

4 Make up six Latin sentences using some of the words listed below. Write out each sentence and then translate it. Include *two* sentences which do not contain nominatives.

nominatives	accusatives	datives	verbs
senātor	flōrēs	fīliae	emō
centuriōnēs	dōna	uxōrī	emit
prīnceps	gladiōs	mīlitibus	emunt
nūntius	fēlem	agricolae	ostendō
amīcī	plaustra	dominō	ostendit
marītus	vīnum	hospitibus	ostendunt
puella	cibum	fēminīs	dat
iuvenēs	epistulās	imperātōrī	damus
virī	fūrem	carnificibus	dant
ancillae	cēram	servīs	trādit
			trāditis
			trādunt

Travel and communication

Judged by modern Western standards, travelling in the Roman world was neither easy nor comfortable; nevertheless, people travelled extensively and there was much movement of goods throughout the provinces of the empire. This was made possible by a remarkable network of straight, well-surfaced roads which connected all major towns by the shortest possible routes. Travellers went on horseback, or used carts or other wheeled vehicles, or they walked. Such journeys were limited by the freshness of horse or traveller. They could cover 60 70 km (40 50 miles) in a day by carriage, perhaps 35 km (25 miles) on foot.

The line of a Roman road was first laid out by surveyors. By taking sightings from high points using smoke from fires, it was possible to ensure that each section of road took the shortest practicable distance between the points. River valleys and impassable mountains forced the roads to make diversions, but once past the obstructions, the roads usually continued along their original line. After the line had been chosen, an embankment of

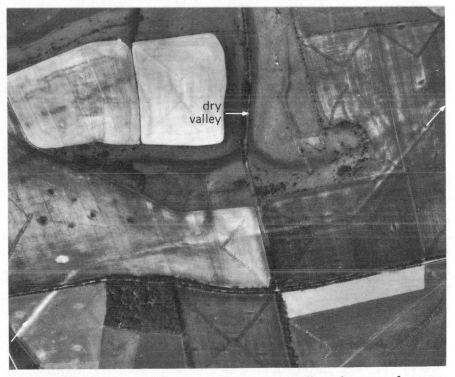

Aerial photograph of a Roman road, showing a diversion round a steep-sided valley

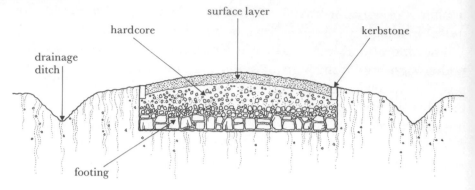

Cross-section showing structure of a Roman road

earth, called an 'agger', was raised to act as a firm foundation. An agger could be as high as 1.2–1.5 metres (4–5 feet). In this was embedded a footing of large stones. This was covered with a layer of smaller stones, rubble and hardcore, and the surface was faced with local materials: large flat stones, small flints or slag from iron mines. This final surface is known as metalling and was curved or 'cambered' to provide effective drainage. On either side of the agger, ditches were dug for the same purpose. Roman road-building was generally carried out with great skill and thoroughness, and the remains of a number of roads still exist today. Many modern roads still follow the Roman alignments and these can be seen very clearly on Ordnance Survey maps.

The roads' original purpose was to allow rapid movement of Roman troops and so ensure military control of the provinces. Other travellers included Roman government officials, who made use of a system known as the Imperial Post (cursus pūblicus). A traveller with a government warrant (diplōma) who was making a journey on official business was supplied with fresh horses at posting stations which were sited at frequent intervals along all main roads; every effort was made to speed such a traveller on his way. In particular, the cursus publicus was used for carrying government correspondence. It has been estimated that by means of the cursus publicus an official message could travel from Britain to Rome (a distance of some 1800 kilometres, 1100 miles) in about seven days. Private letters carried by a person's own slave took much longer.

Travellers would break long journeys with overnight stays at roadside inns. These were, for the most part, small, dirty and uncomfortable, and were frequented by thieves, prostitutes and drunks. The innkeepers, too, were often dishonest. The poet Horace, describing his stay at one inn, comments tersely: 'perfidus hic caupō'. Well-to-do travellers would try to avoid using these inns by arranging to stay with friends or acquaintances, where possible.

Relief showing a Roman light-weight carriage approaching a mile stone

Travelling by sea was generally more popular, although it was restricted to the sailing season (March to November) and was fraught with danger from pirates, storms and shipwrecks. Most sea journeys were undertaken on merchant ships; passenger shipping as we know it did not exist, except for the occasional ferry. A traveller could either hire a boat or wait until a merchant ship was about to put to sea and bargain with the captain for an acceptable fare.

Words and phrases checklist

adstō, adstāre, adstitī – stand by
auctōritās, auctōritātis – authority
audāx, *gen.* audācis – bold, daring
carcer, carceris – prison
colloquium, colloquiī – talk, chat
comprehendō, comprehendere, comprehendī, comprehēnsus –
  arrest
cōnscendō, cōnscendere, cōnscendī – climb on, mount
cum – when
dēscendō, dēscendere, dēscendī – go down, come down
dēserō, dēserere, dēseruī, dēsertus – desert
ēgressus, ēgressa, ēgressum – having gone out
eques, equitis – horseman
flūmen, flūminis – river
humī – on the ground
īnfestus, īnfesta, īnfestum – hostile
intereā – meanwhile
magnopere – greatly
  maximē – very greatly, most of all
neque . . . neque – neither . . . nor
nusquam – nowhere
oppugnō, oppugnāre, oppugnāvī, oppugnātus – attack
passus, passa, passum – having suffered
patefaciō, patefacere, patefēcī, patefactus – reveal
perfidus, perfida, perfidum – treacherous, untrustworthy
pōns, pontis – bridge
rīpa, rīpae – river bank
tantum – only
trānseō, trānsīre, trānsiī – cross
trīstis, trīste – sad
vērum, vērī – the truth

mīlitēs

mīles legiōnis secundae per castra ambulābat. subitō iuvenem ignōtum prope horreum latentem cōnspexit.

'heus tū', clāmāvit mīles, 'quis es?' iuvenis nihil respondit.

mīles iuvenem iterum rogāvit quis esset. iuvenis fūgit.

mīles iuvenem petīvit et facile superāvit. 'furcifer!' exclāmāvit. 'quid prope horreum facis?'

iuvenis dīcere nōlēbat quid prope horreum faceret. mīles eum ad centuriōnem dūxit.

centuriō, iuvenem cōnspicātus, 'hunc agnōscō!' inquit. 'explōrātor
Britannicus est, quem saepe prope castra cōnspexī. quō modō eum
cēpistī?'
tum mīles explicāvit quō modō iuvenem cēpisset.

centuriō, ad iuvenem conversus, 'cūr in castra vēnistī?' rogāvit.
iuvenis tamen tacēbat.
centuriō, ubi cognōscere nōn poterat cūr iuvenis in castra vēnisset,
mīlitem iussit eum ad carcerem dūcere.

iuvenis, postquam verba centuriōnis audīvit, 'ego sum Vercobrix',
inquit, 'fīlius prīncipis Deceanglōrum. vōbīs nōn decōrum est mē in
carcere tenēre.' 'fīlius prīncipis Deceanglōrum?' exclāmāvit
centuriō. 'libentissimē tē videō. nōs tē diū quaerimus, cellamque
optimam tibi in carcere parāvimus.'

Strȳthiō

optiō per castra ambulat. Strȳthiōnem, iam ad castra regressum, cōnspicit.

optiō: heus Strȳthiō! hūc venī! tibi aliquid dīcere volō.

Strȳthiō: nōlī mē vexāre! occupātus sum. Modestum quaerō, quod
           puella eum exspectat. hercle! puellam pulchriōrem
           numquam vīdī. vōx eius est suāvissima; oculī eius . . .   5

optiō: mī Strȳthiō, quamquam occupātissimus es, dēbēs
           maximā cum dīligentiā mē audīre. ā centuriōne nostrō
           missus sum. centuriō tē iubet ad carcerem statim
           festīnāre.

Strȳthiō: īnsānit centuriō! innocēns sum.   1

optiō: tacē! centuriō Modestum quoque iussit ad carcerem
           festīnāre.

Strȳthiō: deōs testēs faciō. innocentēs sumus. nūllum facinus
           commīsimus.

optiō: caudex! tacē! difficile est rem tibi explicāre! Valerius,   1
           centuriō noster, vōs ambōs carcerem custōdīre iussit.

Strȳthiō: nōlī mē vituperāre! rem nunc intellegō! Valerius nōs vult
           custōdēs carceris esse. decōrum est Valeriō nōs ēligere,
           quod fortissimī sumus. ego et Modestus, cum in Āfricā
           mīlitārēmus, sōlī tōtam prōvinciam custōdiēbāmus.   2

optiō: quamquam fortissimī estis, dīligentiam quoque
           maximam praestāre dēbētis. nam inter captīvōs est
           Vercobrix, iuvenis magnae dignitātis, cuius pater est
           prīnceps Deceanglōrum. necesse est vōbīs Vercobrigem
           dīligentissimē custōdīre.   2

optiō *optio (military officer, ranking below centurion)*
castra *camp*
ambōs: ambō *both*
prōvinciam: prōvincia *province*
praestāre *show, display*
captīvōs: captīvus *prisoner, captive*
cuius *whose (genitive of* quī)

Strȳthiō: nōlī anxius cssc, mī optiō. nōbīs nihil difficile est, quod
fortissimī sumus, ut anteā dīxī. tū redī ad Valerium. dīc
Valeriō haec omnia verba. nōlī quicquam omittere!
'Strȳthiō, mīles legiōnis secundae, Valeriō, centuriōnī
legiōnis secundae, salūtem plūrimam dīcit. optiō, ā tē 30
missus, mandāta tua nōbīs tulit. nōs mandātīs tuīs
pārentēs, ad statiōnem prōcēdimus.'

exeunt. optiō centuriōnem quaerit, Strȳthiō amīcum.

omittere *leave out, omit*
salūtem plūrimam dīcit *sends his best wishes*
pārentēs: pārēre *obey*
statiōnem: statiō *post*

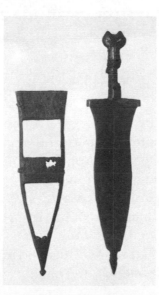

Modestus custōs

Modestus et Strȳthiō, carcerem ingressī, cellās in quibus captīvī
erant īnspiciēbant. habēbat Strȳthiō libellum in quō nōmina
captīvōrum scrīpta erant. Modestus eum rogāvit in quā cellā
Vercobrix inclūsus esset. Strȳthiō, libellum īnspiciēns, cognōvit ubi
Vercobrix iacēret, et Modestum ad cellam dūxit. Modestus, cum ad 5
portam cellae advēnisset, haesitāns cōnstitit.

Strȳthiō 'num cellam intrāre timēs?' inquit. 'vīnctus est fīlius
prīncipis Deceanglōrum. tē laedere nōn potest.'

cum Strȳthiō haec dīxisset, Modestus īrātus exclāmāvit,

'caudex, prīncipis fīlium nōn timeō! cōnstitī quod tē 10
exspectābam. volō tē mihi portam aperīre!'

cum portam Strȳthiō aperuisset, Modestus rūrsus haesitāvit.

'obscūra est cella', inquit Modestus anxius. 'fer mihi lucernam.'

Strȳthiō, vir summae patientiae, lucernam tulit amīcōque
trādidit. ille, cellam ingressus, ē cōnspectū discessit. 15

in angulō cellae iacēbat Vercobrix. Modestus, cum eum vīdisset,
gladium dēstrīnxit. tum, ad mediam cellam prōgressus,
Vercobrigem vituperāre coepit. Vercobrix tamen contumēliās
Modestī audīre nōn poterat, quod graviter dormiēbat. Modestus
Vercobrigī dormientī exsultāns appropinquāvit, et gladium ante ōs 20
eius vibrābat. iterum magnā cum vōce eum vituperābat. Strȳthiō,
quī extrā cellam stābat, attonitus erat. nesciēbat enim cūr Modestus
clāmāret. dormiēbat tamen Vercobrix, ignārus clāmōrum Modestī.

subitō arānea, ē tēctō cellae lāpsa, in nāsum Modestī incidit et
trāns ōs cucurrit. Modestus, ab arāneā territus, ē cellā fūgit. 25

'Strȳthiō! Strȳthiō!' clāmāvit. 'claude portam cellae. nōbīs

necesse est summā cum dīligentiā Vercobrigem custōdīre. etiam
arāneae eum adiuvant!'
Strȳthiō cum portam clausisset, Modestum territum rogāvit quid
accidisset.   30
'Modeste', inquit, 'quam pallidus es! num captīvum timēs?'
'minimē! pallidus sum, quod nōn cēnāvī', respondit.
'vīsne mē ad culīnam īre et tibi cēnam ferre?' rogāvit Strȳthiō.
'optimum cōnsilium est!' inquit alter. 'tū tamen hīc manē. melius
est mihi ipsī ad culīnam īre, quod coquus decem dēnāriōs mihi 35
dēbet.'
haec locūtus, ad culīnam statim cucurrit.

cōnstitit: cōnsistere *halt, stop*
vīnctus: vincīre *bind, tie up*
lucernam: lucerna *lamp*
patientiae: patientia *patience*
cōnspectū: cōnspectus *sight*
angulō: angulus *corner*
prōgressus *having advanced*
contumēliās: contumēlia *insult, abuse*
ante ōs eius *in front of his face*
ignārus *not knowing, unaware*
arānea *spider*
tēctō: tēctum *ceiling, roof*
lāpsa: lapsus *having fallen*
trāns *across*
pallidus *pale*
hīc *here*

About the language

1 In Unit I, you met sentences like this:

'quis clāmōrem audīvit?'   'ubi est captīvus?'
'Who heard the shout?'   'Where is the prisoner?'

In each example, a question is being *asked*. These examples are known as *direct* questions.

2 In Stage 25, you have met sentences like this:

centuriō nesciēbat quis clāmōrem audīvisset.
The centurion did not know who had heard the shout.

equitēs cognōvērunt ubi captīvus esset.
The horsemen found out where the prisoner was.

In each of these examples, the question is not being asked, but is being *reported* or *mentioned*. These examples are known as *indirect* questions. The verb in an indirect question in Latin is normally subjunctive.

3 Compare the following examples:

direct questions	*indirect questions*
'quid Vercobrix fēcit?'	mīlitēs intellēxērunt quid Vercobrix fēcisset.
'What has Vercobrix done?'	The soldiers understood what Vercobrix had done.
'cūr Britannī fūgērunt?'	optiō rogāvit cūr Britannī fūgissent.
'Why did the Britons run away?'	The optio asked why the Britons had run away.
'quis appropinquat?'	custōs nesciēbat quis appropinquāret.
'Who is approaching?'	The guard did not know who was approaching.

4   Further examples of direct and indirect questions:

1 'quis puerum interfēcit?'
2 nēmō sciēbat quis puerum interfēcisset.
3 Salvius tandem intellēxit quō Quīntus et Dumnorix fūgissent.
4 nūntius scīre voluit ubi rēx habitāret.
5 'quō modō pecūniam invēnistī?'
6 iūdex mē rogāvit quō modō pecūniam invēnissem.
7 Salvius nesciēbat cūr Quīntus rēgem adiūvisset.
8 Salvius nesciēbat cūr Quīntus rēgem adiuvāret.

Modestus perfuga

I

Modestus, ēgressus ē culīnā ubi cēnam optimam cōnsūmpserat, ad carcerem redībat. cum ambulāret, sīc cōgitābat,
    'numquam cēnam meliōrem gustāvī; numquam vīnum suāvius bibī. sollicitus tamen sum. nam coquus illam cēnam et mihi et Strȳthiōnī parāvit, sed ego sōlus cōnsūmpsī. nunc mihi necesse est 5 hanc rem Strȳthiōnī explicāre. fortūna tamen mihi favet, quod Strȳthiō est vir magnae patientiae, minimīque cibī.'

perfuga *deserter*
et . . . et *both . . . and*

ubi carcerī appropinquāvit, portam apertam vīdit.

'dī immortālēs!' clāmāvit permōtus. 'Strȳthiō, num portam carceris apertam relīquistī? nēminem neglegentiōrem quam tē nōvī.' 10 carcerem ingressus, portās omnium cellārum apertās invēnit. cum hoc vīdisset, exclāmāvit,

'ēheu! omnēs portae apertae sunt! captīvī, ē cellīs ēlāpsī, omnēs fūgērunt!'

Modestus rem anxius cōgitāvit. nesciēbat enim quō captīvī 15 fūgissent; intellegere nōn poterat cūr Strȳthiō abesset.

'quid facere dēbeō? perīculōsum est hīc manēre ubi mē centuriō invenīre potest. ūna est spēs salūtis. mihi fugiendum est. ō Strȳthiō, Strȳthiō! coēgistī mē statiōnem dēserere. mē perfugam fēcistī. sed deōs testēs faciō. invītus statiōnem dēserō, invītus centuriōnis īram 20 fugiō.'

permōtus *alarmed, disturbed*   spēs *hope*   īram: īra *anger*

II

Modestus, haec locūtus, subitō sonitum audīvit. aliquis portam cellae Vercobrigis aperīre et exīre temptābat!

'mihi ē carcere fugiendum est', aliquis ē cellā clāmāvit.

Modestus, cum haec audīvisset, ad portam cellae cucurrit et
clausit.   5

'Vercobrix, tibi in cellā manendum est!' clāmāvit Modestus.
'euge! nōn effūgit Vercobrix! eum captīvum habeō! euge! nunc mihi
centuriō nocēre nōn potest, quod captīvum summae dignitātis in
carcere retinuī.'

Modestus autem anxius manēbat; nesciēbat enim quid Strȳthiōnī 10
accidisset. subitō pugiōnem humī relictum cōnspexit.

'heus, quid est? hunc pugiōnem agnōscō! est pugiō Strȳthiōnis!
Strȳthiōnī dedī, ubi diem nātālem celebrābat. ēheu! cruentus est
pugiō. ō mī Strȳthiō! nunc rem intellegō. mortuus es! captīvī, ē cellīs
ēlāpsī, tē necāvērunt. ēheu! cum ego tuam cēnam in culīnā 15
cōnsūmerem, illī tē oppugnābant! ō Strȳthiō! nēmō īnfēlīcior est
quam ego. nam tē amābam sīcut pater fīlium. tū tamen nōn inultus
periistī. Vercobrix, quī in hāc cellā etiam nunc manet, poenās dare
dēbet. heus! Vercobrix, mē audī! tibi moriendum est, quod Strȳthiō
meus mortuus est.'   20

haec locūtus, in cellam furēns irrūpit. captīvum, quī intus latēbat,
verberāre coepit.

captīvus: Modeste! mī Modeste! dēsine mē verberāre! nōnne mē
            agnōscis? Strȳthiō sum, quem tū amās sīcut pater
            fīlium.   29

Modestus: Strȳthiō? Strȳthiō! num vīvus es? cūr vīvus es? sceleste!
            furcifer! ubi sunt captīvī quōs custōdiēbās?

Strȳthiō: fūgērunt, Modeste. mē dēcēpērunt. coēgērunt mē
            portās omnium cellārum aperīre.

Modestus: ēheu! quid facere dēbēmus?   30

Strȳthiō: nōbīs statim ē carcere fugiendum est; centuriōnem
            appropinquantem audiō.

Modestus: ō Strȳthiō! ō, quam īnfēlīx sum!

Strȳthiō: nōlī dēspērāre. cōnsilium habeō. tibi necesse est mihi
            cōnfīdere.   35

amīcī ē carcere quam celerrimē fūgērunt.

aliquis *someone*	inultus *unavenged*
relictum: relinquere *leave*	tibi moriendum est *you must die*
cruentus *covered in blood*	vīvus *alive, living*

About the language

1 The examples of the imperfect and pluperfect subjunctive that you have met so far have nearly all ended in '-t' or '-nt', meaning 'he . . .' or 'they . . .':

nēmō sciēbat ubi Britannī **latērent**.
Nobody knew where the Britons were lying hidden.

centuriō, cum hoc **audīvisset**, saeviēbat.
When the centurion had heard this, he was furious.

2 The imperfect and pluperfect subjunctive can also end in '-m', '-mus', '-s' or '-tis', meaning 'I . . .', 'we . . .' or 'you . . .':

custōdēs nōs rogāvērunt cūr **clāmārēmus**.
The guards asked us why we were shouting.

cum patrem **excitāvissem**, ad cubiculum rediī.
When I had awakened my father, I returned to my bedroom.

3 Further examples:

1 nesciēbam quō fūgissēs.
2 cum in Britanniā mīlitārem, oppidum Aquās Sūlis saepe vīsitāvī.
3 cum cēnam tuam cōnsūmerēs, centuriō tē quaerēbat.
4 cum nōmina recitāvissem, hospitēs ad rēgem dūxī.
5 amīcus meus cognōscere voluit ubi habitārētis.
6 puella nōs rogāvit cūr rem tam difficilem suscēpissēmus.

4 The imperfect and pluperfect tenses of the subjunctive are set out in full on page 172 in the Language Information section.

Practising the language

1 Study the form and meaning of the following nouns and give the meaning of the untranslated ones:

deus	god	dea	goddess
fīlius	son	fīlia	
ursus		ursa	she-bear
lupus		lupa	
leō		leaena	
captīvus	prisoner (male)	captīva	
avus	grandfather	avia	
saltātor	dancer	saltātrīx	dancing-girl
vēnātor	hunter	vēnātrīx	
victor		victrīx	winner (female)

Give the meaning of the following nouns:

rēgīna, domina, equa, nūntia

2 Complete the sentences of this story with the most suitable word from the list below, and then translate.

clāmāvit, cucurrit, invēnit, coxit, bibit, cōnsūmpsit, exiit

Modestus ad culīnam īrātus . . . . . culīnam ingressus, coquum occupātum . . . . . . coquus cibum parābat.
    'ubi sunt dēnāriī quōs mihi dēbēs?' . . . . . Modestus.
    coquus, ubi Modestum īrātum vīdit, eī pōculum vīnī obtulit. Modestus libenter vīnum . . . . . . deinde coquus cēnam . . . . . et Modestō obtulit. Modestus, simulac cēnam gustāvit, avidus . . . . . .
    postrēmō Modestus, optimē cēnātus, ē culīnā ēbrius . . . . ., immemor pecūniae. coquus in culīnā stābat cachinnāns.

3 Translate the following sentences and then, with the help of the tables on pages 160–62 in the Language Information section, change their meaning by turning each nominative into a dative and each dative into a nominative, then translate again.

For example: imperātor rēgibus dōna dedit.
The emperor gave gifts to the kings.
This becomes: rēgēs imperātōrī dōna dedērunt.
The kings gave gifts to the emperor.

Notice that in some sentences, as in the example above, you will have to change the verb from singular to plural, or plural to singular.

1 puella puerō gemmam ostendit.
2 mercātor amīcō dōnum ēmit.
3 servus puellīs respondit.
4 rēx cīvibus haec verba dīxit.
5 puerī cīvī nōn crēdidērunt.
6 mīlitēs fēminīs auxilium dedērunt.
7 custōdēs centuriōnī pecūniam trādidērunt.
8 ego tibi nōn fāvī.

4 This exercise is based on the story 'Modestus custōs' on page 80. Read the story again. Complete each of the sentences below with one of the following groups of words and then translate. Use each group of words once only.

cum Modestus ad culīnam abiisset
cum carcerem intrāvissent
cum arānea dē tēctō dēcidisset
cum lucernam tulisset
cum Modestus gladium vibrāret

1 Modestus et Strȳthiō, ..., cellās captīvōrum īnspiciēbant.
2 Strȳthiō, ..., Modestō trādidit.
3 . . . . ., Vercobrix graviter dormiēbat.
4 . . . . ., Modestus fūgit perterritus.
5 . . . . ., Strȳthiō in carcere mānsit.

5 Complete each sentence with the right word and then translate.

1 medicus puellae . . . . . pōculum dedit. (aegram, aegrae)
2 hospitēs coquum . . . . . laudāvērunt. (callidum, callidō)
3 faber mercātōrī . . . . . dēnāriōs reddidit. (īrātum, īrātō)
4 ancillae dominō . . . . . pārēre nōlēbant. (crūdēlem, crūdēlī)
5 centuriō mīlitēs . . . . . castīgābat. (ignāvōs, ignāvīs)
6 puer stultus nautīs . . . . . crēdidit. (mendācēs, mendācibus)
7 stolās . . . . . emēbat fēmina. (novās, novīs)
8 . . . . . amīcīs pecūniam obtulī. (omnēs, omnibus)

The legionary soldier

The crack troops of the Roman army were the soldiers who served in the legions. They were all Roman citizens and full-time professionals who had signed on for twenty-five years. They were highly trained in the skills of infantry warfare and were often specialists in other things as well. In fact a Roman legion, consisting normally of about 5,000 foot soldiers, was a miniature army in itself, capable of constructing forts and camps, manufacturing its weapons and equipment and building roads. On its staff were engineers, architects, carpenters, smiths, doctors, medical orderlies, clerks and accountants.

Recruitment

When he joined the army a new recruit would first be interviewed to ensure that he had the proper legal status, i.e. that he was a Roman citizen; he was also given a medical examination. The army was inclined to favour recruits who came from certain trades, preferring 'blacksmiths, wagon-makers, butchers and huntsmen' and disapproving of 'confectioners, weavers and those who have been employed in occupations appropriate to the women's quarters'.

A legion

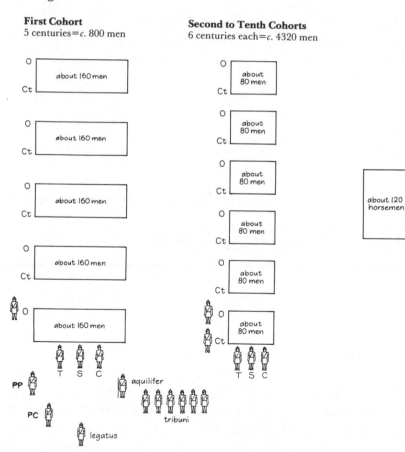

First Cohort
5 centuries=*c.* 800 men

Second to Tenth Cohorts
6 centuries each=*c.* 4320 men

T=tesserarius; S=signifer; C=cornicen (trumpeter); Ct=centurio; O=optio;
PP=primus pilus; PC=praefectus castrorum

Training

After being accepted and sworn in, the new recruit was sent to his unit to begin training. This was thorough, systematic and physically hard. First the young soldier had to learn to march at the regulation pace for distances of up to 24 Roman miles (about 22 statute miles or 35 kilometres). Physical fitness was further developed by running, jumping, swimming and carrying heavy packs. Next came weapon training, starting with a wooden practice-sword and wicker shield. The soldier learned to handle the shield correctly and to attack a dummy target with the point of his sword. When he had mastered the basic skills with dummy weapons he went on to the real thing and finally practised individual combat in pairs, probably with a leather button on the point of his sword.

The second phase of weapon training was to learn to throw the javelin (pīlum). This had a wooden shaft 1.5 metres (5 feet) long and a pointed iron head of 0.6 metres (2 feet). This head was cleverly constructed. The first 25 centimetres (10 inches) were finely tempered to give it penetrating power, but the rest was left untempered so that it was fairly soft and liable to bend. Thus when the javelin was hurled at an enemy, from a distance of 23–28 metres (25–30 yards), its point penetrated and stuck into his shield, while the neck of the metal head bent and the shaft hung down. This not only made the javelin unusable, so that it could not be thrown back, but also made the encumbered shield so difficult to manage that the enemy might have to abandon it altogether.

When he had reached proficiency in handling his weapons and was physically fit, the soldier was ready to leave the barracks for training in the open countryside. This began with route marches on which he carried not only his body armour and weapons but also several days' ration of food, together with equipment for making an overnight camp, such as a saw, an axe and also a basket for moving earth, as shown in the picture below. Much importance was attached to the proper construction of the camp at the end of the day's march, and the young soldier was given careful instruction and practice. Several practice camps and forts have been found in Britain. For example, at Cawthorn in Yorkshire the soldiers under training did rather more than just dig ditches and ramparts; they also constructed platforms for catapults (ballistae) and even built camp ovens.

Relief from Trajan's column showing soldiers building a fort

Work

The fully trained legionary did not spend all or even much of his time on active service. Most of it was spent on peacetime duties, such as building or roadmaking, and, during the first century A.D. at least, he had good prospects of surviving till his discharge. He was generally stationed in a large legionary fortress somewhere near the frontiers of the empire in places such as Deva (Chester), Bonna (Bonn) and Vindobona (Vienna) which were key points in the Roman defences against the barbarians.

Many of the daily duties were the same wherever he was stationed. A duty roster, written on papyrus, has come down to us and lists the names of thirty-six soldiers, all members of the same century in one of the legions stationed in Egypt. It covers the first ten days in October possibly in the year A.D. 87. A selection of the entries is given on page 95 below. For example, C. Julius Valens was to spend October 2nd on guard duty in the tower of the fortress, October 4th repairing boots and October 8th acting as orderly (servant) to one of the officers.

Pay

In both war and peacetime the soldier received the same rate of pay. In the first century A.D., up to the time of the Emperor Domitian (A.D. 81–96), this amounted to 225 denarii per annum; Domitian improved the rate to 300 denarii. These amounts were gross pay, and before any money was handed to the soldier certain deductions were made. Surprising though it may seem, he was obliged to pay for his food, clothing and equipment. He would also leave some money in the military savings bank. What he actually received in cash may have been only a quarter or a fifth of his gross pay. Whether he felt badly treated is difficult to say. Certainly we know of cases of discontent, but pay and conditions of service were apparently not bad enough to discourage recruits. The soldier could look forward to some promotion and eventually an honourable discharge with a gratuity of 3,000 denarii or an allocation of land.

Promotion

If a soldier was promoted his life began to change in several ways. He was paid more and he was exempted from many of the fatigues performed by the ordinary soldier. Each century was commanded by a centurion and he was assisted by an optio who was waiting for a vacancy in the ranks of the centurions. There was also in each century a standard-bearer (signifer), a 'tesserārius' who commanded the guard-pickets and one or two clerks. The centurions, who were roughly equivalent to non-commissioned warrant officers in a modern army, were the backbone of the legion. There were sixty of them, each responsible for the training and discipline of a century, and their importance was reflected in their pay, which was probably about 1,500 denarii per annum. Most of them had risen from the ranks by virtue of courage and ability. The senior centurion of the legion (prīmus pīlus) was a highly respected figure; he was at least fifty years old and had worked his way up through the various grades of centurion. He held office for one year, then received a large gratuity and was allowed to retire; or he might go on still further to become 'praefectus castrōrum' (commander of the camp).

Senior officers

The men mentioned so far would expect to spend the whole of their working lives serving as professional soldiers. The senior officers, on the other hand, spent a much shorter period of time in the legion, possibly three or four years, without any previous service as centurion or ordinary legionary.

The officer commanding the legion was called a 'lēgātus'. He was a member of the Senate in Rome and usually fairly young, in his middle thirties. He was assisted by six military tribunes. Of these, one was usually a young man of noble birth, serving his military apprenticeship before starting a political career. The other five were members of a slightly lower social class (equitēs) and they too would be in their thirties. They were generally able, wealthy and educated men, often aiming at important posts in the imperial civil service.

	1 Oct.	2 Oct.	3 Oct.	4 Oct.	5 Oct.	6 Oct.	7 Oct.	8 Oct.	9 Oct.	10 Oct.
C. Julius Valens	training arena	tower	drainage	boots	armoury	armoury	baths	orderly	in century	baths
L. Sextilius Germanus	gate guard	standards	baths	tower	← duty in D. Decrius' century →					
M. Antonius Crispus	baths	stretchers	in century	plain clothes	in century	—	← tribune's escort →			
T. Flavius	—	—	—	baths	baths	baths	gate guard	—	—	—
M. Domitius	—	—	← detachment to the granaries at Neapolis →							

Words and phrases checklist

accidō, accidere, accidī – happen
aliquis – someone
aperiō, aperīre, aperuī, apertus – open
autem – but
captīvus, captīvī – prisoner, captive
castra, castrōrum – camp
cōgō, cōgere, coēgī, coāctus – force, compel
dēpōnō, dēpōnere, dēposuī, dēpositus – put down, take off
dēsinō, dēsinere – end, cease
dignitās, dignitātis – importance, prestige
dīligentia, dīligentiae – industry, hard work
explicō, explicāre, explicāvī, explicātus – explain
extrā – outside
furēns, *gen.* furentis – furious, in a rage
haesitō, haesitāre, haesitāvī – hesitate
immemor, *gen.* immemoris – forgetful
immortālis, immortāle – immortal
    dī immortālēs! – heavens above!
laedō, laedere, laesī, laesus – harm
lateō, latēre, latuī – lie hidden
legiō, legiōnis – legion
nescio, nescīre, nescīvī – not know
nōmen, nōminis – name
ōs, ōris – face
poena, poenae – punishment
    poenās dare – pay the penalty, be punished
rūrsus – again
scelestus, scelesta, scelestum – wicked
statiō, statiōnis – post
suāvis, suāve – sweet
testis, testis – witness

Agricola

adventus Agricolae

mīlitēs legiōnis secundae, quī Dēvae in castrīs erant, diū et strēnuē labōrābant. nam Gāius Iūlius Sīlānus, lēgātus legiōnis, adventum Agricolae exspectābat. mīlitēs, ā centuriōnibus iussī, multa et varia faciēbant. aliī arma poliēbant; aliī aedificia pūrgābant; aliī plaustra reficiēbant. Sīlānus neque quiētem neque commeātum mīlitibus 5 dedit.

mīlitēs, ignārī adventūs Agricolae, rem graviter ferēbant. trēs continuōs diēs labōrāvērunt; quārtō diē Sīlānus adventum Agricolae nūntiāvit. mīlitēs, cum hoc audīvissent, maximē gaudēbant quod Agricolam dīligēbant. 10

tertiā hōrā Sīlānus mīlitēs in ōrdinēs longōs īnstrūxit, ut Agricolam salūtārent. mīlitēs, cum Agricolam castra intrantem vīdissent, magnum clāmōrem sustulērunt.

'iō, Agricola! iō, iō, Agricola!'

Agricola ad tribūnal prōcessit ut pauca dīceret. omnēs statim 15 tacuērunt ut contiōnem Agricolae audīrent.

'gaudeō', inquit, 'quod hodiē vōs rūrsus videō. nūllam legiōnem fidēliōrem habeō, nūllam fortiōrem. disciplīnam studiumque vestrum valdē laudō.'

mīlitēs ita hortātus, per ōrdinēs prōcessit ut eōs īnspiceret. deinde 20 prīncipia intrāvit ut colloquium cum Sīlānō habēret.

adventus *arrival*	quārtō diē *on the fourth day*
Dēvae *at Chester*	gaudēbant: gaudēre *be pleased, rejoice*
strēnuē *hard, energetically*	tertiā hōrā *at the third hour*
aliī . . . aliī . . . aliī *some . . . others*	iō! *hurray!*
. . . *others*	tribūnal *platform*
arma *arms, weapons*	contiōnem: contiō *speech*
poliēbant: polīre *polish*	disciplīnam: disciplīna *discipline,*
pūrgābant: pūrgāre *clean*	*orderliness*
quiētem: quiēs *rest*	studium *enthusiasm, keenness*
commeātum: commeātus *leave*	vestrum: vester *your*
trēs . . . diēs *for three days*	hortātus *having encouraged*
continuōs: continuus *continuous, on end*	prīncipia *headquarters*

When you have read this story, answer the questions at the end.

in prīncipiīs

Salvius ipse paulō prius ad castra advēnerat. iam in legiōnis secundae prīncipiīs sedēbat, Agricolam anxius exspectāns. sollicitus erat quod in epistulā, quam ad Agricolam mīserat, multa falsa scrīpserat. in prīmīs Cogidubnum sēditiōnis accūsāverat. in animō volvēbat num Agricola sibi crēditūrus esset. Belimicum 5 sēcum dūxerat ut testis esset.

subitō Salvius, Agricolam intrantem cōnspicātus, ad eum festīnāvit ut salūtāret. deinde renovāvit ea quae in epistulā scrīpserat. Agricola, cum haec audīvisset, diū tacuit. dēnique maximē commōtus, 10
'quanta perfidia!' inquit. 'quanta īnsānia! id quod mihi patefēcistī, vix intellegere possum. īnsānīvit Cogidubnus. īnsānīvērunt prīncipēs Rēgnēnsium. numquam nōs oportet barbarīs crēdere; tūtius est eōs omnēs prō hostibus habēre. nunc mihi necesse est rēgem opprimere quem quīnque annōs prō amīcō 15 habeō.'

haec locūtus, ad Sīlānum, lēgātum legiōnis, sē vertit.
'Sīlāne', inquit, 'nōs oportet rēgem prīncipēsque Rēgnēnsium quam celerrimē opprimere. tibi statim cum duābus cohortibus proficīscendum est.' 20

Sīlānus, ē prīncipiīs ēgressus, centuriōnibus mandāta dedit. eōs iussit cohortēs parāre. intereā Agricola plūra dē rēgis perfidiā rogāre coepit. Salvius eī respondit,

paulō prius *a little earlier*	īnsānia *madness, insanity*
in prīmīs *in particular*	nōs oportet *we must*
sēditiōnis: sēditiō *rebellion*	prō hostibus habēre *reckon as enemies*
in animō volvēbat: in animō volvere	opprimere *crush*
wonder, turn over in the mind	tibi . . . proficīscendum est *you must*
num *whether*	*set out*
crēditūrus *going to believe*	cohortibus: cohors *cohort*
renovāvit: renovāre *repeat, renew*	

'ecce Belimicus, vir ingeniī optimī summaeque fideī, quem iste
Cogidubnus corrumpere temptābat. Belimicus autem, quī 2
blanditiās rēgis spernēbat, omnia mihi patefēcit.'

'id quod Salvius dīxit vērum est', inquit Belimicus. 'rēx Rōmānōs
ōdit. Rōmānōs ē Britanniā expellere tōtamque īnsulam occupāre
cupit. nāvēs igitur comparat. mīlitēs exercet. etiam bēstiās saevās
colligit. nūper bēstiam in mē impulit ut mē interficeret.' 3

Agricola tamen hīs verbīs diffīsus, Salvium dīligentius rogāvit
quae indicia sēditiōnis vīdisset. cognōscere voluit quot essent
armātī, num Britannī cīvēs Rōmānōs interfēcissent, quās urbēs
dēlēvissent.

subitō magnum clāmōrem omnēs audīvērunt. per iānuam 3
prīncipiōrum perrūpit homō squālidus. ad Agricolam praeceps
cucurrit genibusque eius haesit.

'cīvis Rōmānus sum', inquit. 'Quīntum Caecilium Iūcundum mē
vocant. ego multās iniūriās passus hūc tandem advēnī. hoc ūnum
dīcere volō. Cogidubnus est innocēns.' 4

haec locūtus humī prōcubuit exanimātus.

corrumpere *corrupt*
blanditiās: blanditiae *flatteries*
spernēbat: spernere *despise, reject*
diffīsus *having distrusted*
indicia: indicium *sign, evidence*
armātī: armātus *armed*
perrūpit: perrumpere *burst through, burst in*
squālidus *covered in dirt, filthy*

1 Why has Salvius come to Chester?
2 Why has he brought Belimicus with him?
3 Why do you think Agricola stays silent for a long time (line 9)?
4 What orders does he give to Silanus?
5 Why does Agricola feel doubtful about Belimicus' statement?
6 What questions does Agricola put to Salvius? Would Salvius find
   Agricola's questions easy to answer? Do you think Agricola ought
   to have asked these questions *before* sending out the cohorts?
7 What happens before Salvius can answer Agricola?
8 What is the first thing Quintus says? Why does he say this first?

About the language

1   Study the following examples:

mīlitēs ad prīncipia convēnērunt **ut Agricolam audīrent**.
The soldiers gathered at the headquarters in order that they might hear Agricola.

per tōtam noctem labōrābat medicus **ut vulnera mīlitum sānāret**.
The doctor worked all night in order that he might treat the soldiers' wounds.

The groups of words in heavy print are known as *purpose clauses*, because they indicate the *purpose* for which an action was done. For instance, in the second example above, the group of words 'ut vulnera mīlitum sānāret' indicates the purpose of the doctor's work. The verb in a purpose clause in Latin is always subjunctive.

2   Further examples:

1 dominus stilum et cērās poposcit ut epistulam scrīberet.
2 omnēs cīvēs ad silvam contendērunt ut leōnem mortuum spectārent.
3 dēnique ego ad patrem rediī ut rem explicārem.
4 pugiōnem rapuī ut captīvum interficerem.

3   Instead of translating 'ut' and the subjunctive as 'in order that he (they) might . . .', it is often possible to use a simpler form of words:

mīlitēs ad prīncipia convēnērunt ut Agricolam audīrent.
The soldiers gathered at the headquarters in order to hear Agricola.
     or, simpler still:
The soldiers gathered at the headquarters to hear Agricola.

tribūnus

Agricola, ubi hoc vīdit, custōdēs iussit Quīntum auferre medicumque arcessere. tum ad tribūnum mīlitum, quī adstābat, sē vertit.

'mī Rūfe', inquit, 'prūdentissimus es omnium tribūnōrum quōs habeō. tē iubeō hunc hominem summā cum cūrā interrogāre.'

Salvius, cum Rūfus exiisset, valdē commōtus,

'cūr tempus terimus?' inquit. 'omnia explicāre possum. nōtus est mihi hic homō. nūper in vīllā mē vīsitāvit, quamquam nōn invītāveram. trēs mēnsēs apud mē mānsit, opēs meās dēvorāns. duōs tripodās argenteōs habēbam, quōs abstulit ut Cogidubnō daret. sed eum nōn accūsāvī, quod hospes erat. ubi tamen Aquās Sūlis mēcum advēnit, facinus scelestum committere temptāvit. venēnum parāvit ut Memorem, haruspicem Rōmānum, necāret. postquam rem nōn effēcit, mē ipsum accūsāvit. nōlī eī crēdere.

multō perfidior est quam Britannī.' 15
    haec cum audīvisset, Agricola respondit,
    'sī tālia fēcit, eī moriendum est.'
    mox revēnit Rūfus valdē attonitus.
    'Quīntus Caecilius', inquit, 'est iuvenis summae fideī. patrem
meum, quem Alexandrīae relīquī, bene nōverat. hoc prō certō 20
habeō quod Quīntus hanc epistulam mihi ostendit, ā patre ipsō
scrīptam.'
    Agricola statim Quīntum ad sē vocāvit, cēterōsque dīmīsit.
Salvius, Quīntum dētestātus, anxius exiit. Agricola cum Quīntō
colloquium trēs hōrās habēbat. 25

tribūnus *tribune (high-ranking officer)*	dēvorāns: dēvorāre *devour, eat up*
prūdentissimus: prūdēns *shrewd, intelligent*	multō perfidior *much more treacherous*
	tālia *such things*
tempus terimus: tempus terere *waste time*	prō certō habeō: prō certō habēre *know for certain*
opēs *money, wealth*	dētestātus *having cursed*

About the language

1 From Stage 14 onwards you have met sentences of this kind:

    necesse est mihi cēnam parāre.   I must prepare the dinner.
    necesse est vōbīs labōrāre.   You must work.

2 You have now met another way of expressing the same idea:

    necesse est nōbīs currere. ⎫
    nōbīs **currendum** est. ⎭   We must run.

    necesse est eī revenīre. ⎫
    eī **reveniendum** est. ⎭   He must come back.

The word in heavy print is known as the *gerundive*.

3 Further examples:

    1 mihi fugiendum est.
    2 nōbīs ambulandum est.
    3 tibi hīc manendum est.
    4 omnibus servīs labōrandum est.

contentiō

Agricola, cum Quīntum audīvisset, vehementer saeviēbat. Salvium furēns arcessīvit. quī, simulatque intrāvit, aliquid dīcere coepit. Agricola tamen, cum silentium iussisset, Salvium vehementer accūsāvit.

'dī immortālēs! Cogidubnus est innocēns, tū perfidus. cūr tam īnsānus eram ut tibi crēderem? quīnque annōs hanc prōvinciam iam administrō. rēgem Cogidubnum bene cognōvī. saepe rēx mihi auxiliō fuit. neque perfidum neque mendācem umquam sē praestitit. cūr tū crīmen falsum in eum intulistī? accūsāvistīne eum ut potentiam tuam augērēs? simulatque ad hanc prōvinciam vēnistī, amīcī mē dē calliditāte tuā monuērunt. nunc rēs ipsa mē docuit. num Imperātor Domitiānus hanc tantam perfidiam ferre potest? ego sānē nōn possum. in hāc prōvinciā summam potestātem habeō. iubeō tē hās inimīcitiās dēpōnere. iubeō tē ad Cogidubnī aulam īre, veniamque ab eō petere. praetereā tē oportet Imperātōrī ipsī rem explicāre.'

haec ubi dīxit Agricola, Salvius respondit īrātus,

'quam caecus es! quam longē errās! tē ipsum oportet Imperātōrī id quod in Britanniā fēcistī explicāre. quīnque annōs hanc prōvinciam pessimē administrās. tū enim in ultimīs Britanniae partibus bellum geris et victōriās inānēs ē Calēdoniā refers; sed Imperātor pecūniās opēsque accipere cupit. itaque rēgnum Cogidubnī occupāre cōnstituit; Calēdoniam floccī nōn facit. tū sānē hoc nescīs. in magnō perīculō es, quod cōnsilium meum spernis. nōn sōlum mihi sed Imperātōrī ipsī obstās.'

cum hanc contentiōnem inter sē habērent, subitō nūntius prīncipia ingressus exclāmāvit,

'mortuus est Cogidubnus!'

auxiliō fuit *was a help, was helpful*
potentiam: potentia *power*
augērēs: augēre *increase*
inimīcitiās: inimīcitia *feud, quarrel*
tē oportet *you must*
caecus *blind*
pessimē *very badly*
victōriās: victōria *victory*
inānēs: inānis *empty, meaningless*
Calēdoniā: Calēdonia *Scotland*
cōnstituit: cōnstituere *decide*

Practising the language

1   Study the form and meaning of the following verbs and nouns, and give the meaning of the untranslated words:

amāre	to love	amor	love
timēre	to be afraid	timor	fear
honōrāre	to honour	honor	
clāmāre		clāmor	
labōrāre		labor	
fulgēre		fulgor	brightness
pavēre	to be alarmed	pavor	
furere		furor	madness, fury
tremere		tremor	a shaking, a tremor
dolēre (1)	to hurt, to be painful	dolor (1)	
dolēre (2)	to be sad	dolor (2)	

Give the meaning of the following nouns:

favor, pallor, sūdor

2   Complete each sentence with the right word and then translate.

1 Agricola, ubi verba . . . . . audīvit, Salvium arcessīvit. (Quīntum, Quīntī, Quīntō)

2 omnēs hospitēs . . . . . saltātrīcis laudāvērunt. (artem, artis, artī)

3 iter nostrum difficile erat, quod tot cīvēs . . . . . complēbant. (viās, viārum, viīs)

4 prō prīncipiīs stābat magna turba . . . . . . (mīlitēs, mīlitum, mīlitibus)

5 lēgātus, postquam mandāta . . . . . dedit, legiōnem ad montem proximum dūxit. (centuriōnēs, centuriōnum, centuriōnibus)

6 iūdex, quī . . . . . nōn crēdēbat, īrātissimus fīēbat. (puerōs, puerōrum, puerīs)

3 Translate each English sentence into Latin by selecting correctly from the list of Latin words.

1 The kind citizens had provided help.

    cīvis   benignī   auxilium   praebuērunt
    cīvēs   benignōs   auxiliī   praebuerant

2 They arrested the soldier in the kitchen of an inn.

    mīlitem   per culīnam   tabernae   comprehendunt
    mīlitis   in culīnā   tabernārum comprehendērunt

3 Master! Read this letter!

    domine   haec   epistula   lege
    dominus   hanc   epistulam   legis

4 The old men departed, praising the brave messenger.

    senēs   discēdunt   fortem   nūntium   laudāns
    senum   discessērunt   fortī   nūntiōs   laudantēs

5 How can we avoid the punishments of the gods?

    quō modō   poenae   deōrum   vītantēs   possumus
    quis   poenās   deīs   vītāre   poterāmus

6 The words of the soothsayer frightened him.

    verbum   haruspicis   eam   eum   terruit
    verba   haruspicī   eōs   terruērunt

4 Complete each sentence with the most suitable word from the list below, and then translate.

epistulam, audīvisset, ēgressus, invēnērunt, equīs, captī

1 Salvius, ē prīncipiīs . . . . ., Belimicum quaesīvit.
2 Agricola, cum haec verba . . . . ., ad Rūfum sē vertit.
3 dominus . . . . . ē manibus servī impatiēns rapuit.
4 custōdēs nūntium humī iacentem . . . . . .
5 quattuor Britannī, in pugnā . . . . ., vītam miserrimam in carcere agēbant.
6 aliī mīlitēs . . . . . aquam dabant, aliī frūmentum in horrea īnferēbant.

Agricola, governor of Britain

With the abbreviated words written out, this reads:
imperatore Vespasiano VIIII Tito imperatore VII consule Cnaeo
Iulio Agricola legato Augusti propraetore.

The two inscriptions above both contain the name of Gnaeus Julius
Agricola. The first comes from a lead water-pipe found at Chester,
the second from the forum of Verulamium (St Albans). These
inscriptions might have been virtually all that we knew about the
man if his life-story had not been written by his son-in-law, the
historian Tacitus. Because of Tacitus' biography we possess a very
detailed picture of Agricola.

He was born on June 13, A.D. 40 in the Roman colony of Forum
Iulii in south-east Gaul. The town had been founded by Julius
Caesar for his veteran soldiers, and most of its inhabitants were
Italian-born citizens rather than native Gauls. (It is today the
French town of Fréjus.) He came from a distinguished family. His
grandfathers had both held important government posts and his
father had been made a senator by the Emperor Tiberius, but later
fell foul of the Emperor Gaius Caligula and was executed in A.D. 40,
shortly after Agricola was born.

Agricola went to school at Massilia (Marseilles), which was the
cultural and educational centre of southern Gaul. He followed the
normal curriculum for the young sons of upper-class Roman

families: public speaking (taught by a 'rhētor') and philosophy. He
enjoyed the latter, but Tacitus records his mother's reaction:
'I remember that Agricola often told us that in his youth he was
more enthusiastic about philosophy than a Roman and a senator
was expected to be, and his mother thought it wise to put a
damper on such a passionate interest.'
At the age of eighteen, Agricola served in the Roman army in
Britain with the rank of 'tribūnus', like Barbillus Rufus in the story
on p. 102. He used this opportunity to become familiar with the
province. The soldiers under his command had a similar
opportunity to get to know him. Two years later, during the revolt of
Boudica in A.D. 60, he witnessed the grim realities of warfare.
Agricola was by now very knowledgeable about the province of
Britain and this knowledge was to stand him in good stead during
his governorship some eighteen years later.
Back in Rome, he continued his political career. In A.D. 70, he
returned to Britain to take command of the Twentieth Legion which
was stationed at Viroconium (Wroxeter) and had become undis-
ciplined and troublesome. His success in handling this difficult task
was rewarded by promotion to the governorship of Aquitania in
Gaul. In A.D. 77 he became consul and the following year returned
to Britain for a third time, as governor of the province. The political
experience and military skill which he had acquired by then
equipped him to face an exciting, if demanding, situation.
Agricola rose to the challenge in many different ways. He actively
promoted a policy of romanisation; he extended a network of roads
and forts across northern Britain, including the legionary fortress at
Chester; and during his governorship he virtually doubled the area
of Roman-held territory in Britain.

Career of Agricola

A.D. 58   Tribunus Militum in Britain
    64   Quaestor in Asia
    66   Tribunus Plebis in Rome
    68   Praetor in Rome
    70   Commander of Twentieth Legion in Britain
    74   Governor of Aquitania
    77   Consul
    78   Governor of Britain

Words and phrases checklist

accūsō, accūsāre, accūsāvī, accūsātus – accuse
auferō, auferre, abstulī, ablātus – take away, steal
bellum, bellī – war
   bellum gerere – wage war, campaign
cohors, cohortis – cohort
colligō, colligere, collēgī, collēctus – gather, collect
commōtus, commōta, commōtum – moved, excited, upset
doceō, docēre, docuī, doctus – teach
facinus, facinoris – crime
falsus, falsa, falsum – false, dishonest
fidēs, fideī – loyalty, trustworthiness
īnsānus, īnsāna, īnsānum – mad, crazy, insane
īnstruō, īnstruere, īnstrūxī, īnstrūctus – draw up
lēgātus, lēgātī – commander
num – whether
occupō, occupāre, occupāvī, occupātus – seize, take over
oportet – it is right
   mē oportet – I must
perfidia, perfidiae – treachery
praebeō, praebēre, praebuī, praebitus – provide
prīncipia, prīncipiōrum – headquarters
prōvincia, prōvinciae – province
quot? – how many?
referō, referre, rettulī, relātus – bring back
rēgnum, rēgnī – kingdom
saevus, saeva, saevum – savage, cruel
sānē – obviously
sī – if
tribūnus, tribūnī – tribune (high-ranking officer)
ultimus, ultima, ultimum – furthest
ut – that, in order that

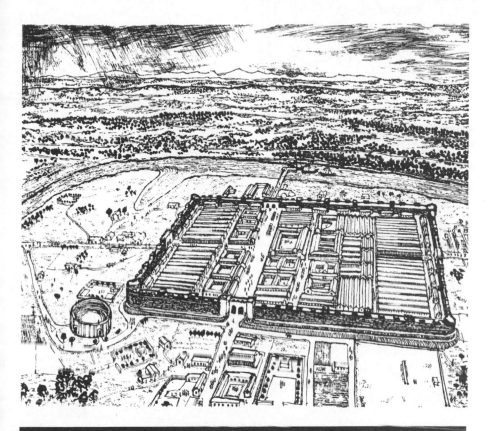

in castrīs

'fuge mēcum ad horreum!'

extrā carcerem, Modestus et Strȳthiō sermōnem anxiī habēbant.
Modestus Strȳthiōnem monēbat ut ad horreum sēcum fugeret.

'invenīte Modestum Strȳthiōnemque!'

prō prīncipiīs, centuriō Valerius mīlitibus mandāta dabat.
centuriō mīlitibus imperābat ut Modestum Strȳthiōnemque invenīrent.

'castra Rōmāna oppugnāte!
horrea incendite!'

in silvā proximā, Vercobrix contiōnem apud Britannōs habēbat.
Vercobrix Britannōs incitābat ut castra Rōmāna oppugnārent et horrea incenderent.

When you have read this story, answer the questions at the end.

sub horreō

Modestus et Strȳthiō, ē carcere ēgressī, ad horreum fūgērunt. per
aditum angustum rēpsērunt et sub horreō cēlātī manēbant. centuriō
Valerius, cum portās cellārum apertās carceremque dēsertum
vīdisset, īrātissimus erat. mīlitibus imperāvit ut Modestum et
Strȳthiōnem caperent. mīlitēs tamen, quamquam per tōta castra 5
quaerēbant, eōs invenīre nōn poterant. illī quīnque diēs mānsērunt
cēlātī. sextō diē Modestus tam miser erat ut rem diūtius ferre nōn
posset.

Modestus: quam īnfēlīx sum! mālim in illō carcere esse potius
          quam sub hōc horreō latēre. quālis est haec vīta? 10
          necesse est mihi grāna quae mūrēs relīquērunt
          cōnsūmere. adest Strȳthiō, comes exiliī, sed mē nōn
          adiuvat. nam Strȳthiō est vir maximī silentiī,
          minimique iocī. ēheu! mē taedet huius vītae.
Strȳthiō: mī Modeste, difficile est nōbīs sub horreō diūtius 15
          manēre. nunc tamen advesperāscit. vīsne mē, ex horreō
          ēgressum, cibum quaerere? hominibus miserrimīs cibus
          sōlācium semper affert.
Modestus: id est cōnsilium optimum. nōbīs cēnandum est.
          Strȳthiō, tē huic reī praeficiō. ī prīmum ad coquum. 20
          eum iubē cēnam splendidam coquere et hūc portāre.
          deinde quaere Aulum et Pūblicum, amīcōs nostrōs!

aditum: aditus *entrance*	exiliī: exilium *exile*
angustum: angustus *narrow*	mē taedet *I am tired, I am bored*
rēpsērunt: rēpere *crawl*	advesperāscit: advesperāscere *get dark,*
imperāvit: imperāre *order, command*	*become dark*
sextō: sextus *sixth*	sōlācium *comfort*
mālim *I should prefer*	affert: afferre *bring*
potius *rather*	praeficiō: praeficere *put in charge*
grāna: grānum *grain*	prīmum *first*

invītā eōs ad cēnam! iubē Aulum amphoram vīnī ferre,
Pūblicum lucernam āleāsque. tum curre ad vīcum;
Nigrīnam quaere! optima est saltātrīcum; mihi 25
saltātrīcēs quoque sōlācium afferunt.

Strȳthiō: quid dīcis? vīsne mē saltātrīcem in castra dūcere?
Modestus: abī caudex!

Strȳthiō, ut mandāta Modestī efficeret, invītus discessit. coquō
persuāsit ut cēnam splendidam parāret; Aulō et Pūblicō persuāsit 30
ut vīnum et lucernam āleāsque ferrent; Nigrīnam ōrāvit ut ad
horreum venīret, sed eī persuādēre nōn poterat.

vīcum: vīcus *town, village*
ōrāvit: ōrāre *beg*

1 What was the purpose of a 'horreum'? Why was its floor raised
above ground level? What does this enable Modestus and
Strythio to do?
2 After five days, what has Modestus been forced to do?
3 What makes Strythio think he can go outside without getting
caught?
4 Who is to bring the dinner to the granary? What are Aulus and
Publicus to bring? Who else is to come to the dinner? Where is she
to be found?
5 Why is Strythio 'invītus' (line 29)? How successful is he in
carrying out Modestus' instructions?
6 Which would you expect to be built first, the 'castra' or the
'vīcus'?

About the language

1 In Unit I, you met sentences like this:

'redīte!' 'pecūniam trāde!'
'Go back!' 'Hand over the money!'

In each example, an order or command is being *given*. These
examples are known as *direct* commands.

2 In Stage 27, you have met sentences like this:

lēgātus mīlitibus imperāvit ut redīrent.
The commander ordered his soldiers that they should go back.
   or, in more natural English:
The commander ordered his soldiers to go back.

latrōnēs mercātōrī imperāvērunt ut pecūniam trāderet.
The robbers ordered the merchant that he should hand over the
money.
   or, in more natural English:
The robbers ordered the merchant to hand over the money

In each of these examples, the command is not being given, but
is being *reported* or *mentioned*. These examples are known as
indirect commands. The verb in an indirect command in Latin is
usually subjunctive.

3 Compare the following examples:

direct commands	*indirect commands*
'contendite!'	iuvenis amīcīs persuāsit ut contenderent.
'Hurry!'	The young man persuaded his friends to hurry.
'dā mihi aquam!'	captīvus custōdem ōrāvit ut aquam sibi daret.
'Give me water!'	The prisoner begged the guard to give him water.
'fuge!'	me monuit ut fugerem
'Run away!'	He warned me to run away.

4 Further examples of direct and indirect commands:

1 nēmō ancillae persuādēre poterat ut saltāret.
2 'tacē!'
3 centuriō mihi imperāvit ut tacērem.
4 vōs saepe monēbam ut dīligenter labōrārētis.
5 'parcite mihi!'
6 senex nōs ōrābat ut sibi parcerēmus.
7 coquus servīs imperāvit ut vīnum in mēnsam pōnerent.
8 comitēs mercātōrem monuērunt ut ab oppidō clam discēderet.

Modestus prōmōtus

cum Strȳthiō cēnam et amīcōs quaereret, decem Britannī ā
Vercobrige ductī, castrīs cautē appropinquābant. Vercobrix enim
eīs persuāserat ut castra oppugnārent. Britannī, postquam custōdēs
vītāvērunt, vallum tacitē trānscendērunt et castra intrāvērunt. in
manibus facēs tenēbant ut horrea incenderent. celeriter ad horrea 5
advēnērunt quod prius cognōverant ubi sita essent.

Modestus, ignārus adventūs Britannōrum, sub horreō sedēbat.
adeō ēsuriēbat ut dē vītā paene dēspērāret. per parvam rīmam
prōspiciēbat, reditum Strȳthiōnis exspectāns.

'trēs hōrās Strȳthiōnem iam exspectō. quid eī accidit?'   10
subitō manum hominum per tenebrās cōnspexit.

'euge! tandem vēnērunt amīcī! heus, amīcī, hūc venīte!'

Britannī, cum Modestī vōcem audīvissent, erant tam attonitī, ut
immōtī stārent. respondēre nōn audēbant. Vercobrix tamen, quī
raucam Modestī vōcem agnōverat, ad comitēs versus,   1.

'nōlīte timēre', inquit susurrāns. 'nōtus est mihi hic mīles. stultior
est quam asinus. nōbīs nocēre nōn potest.'

tum Britannī per aditum tacitī rēpsērunt. simulatque intrāvērunt, Modestus eīs obviam iit, ut salūtāret.

'salvēte, amīcī! nunc nōbīs cēnandum ac bibendum est.'   20
tum Britannus quīdam, vir ingēns, in Modestum incurrit.

'ō Nigrīna, dēliciae meae!' clāmāvit Modestus. 'tē nōn agnōvī!
quam longī sunt capillī tuī! age! cōnsīde prope mē! dā mihi ōsculum!
quis lucernam habet?'

Vercobrix, cum Modestum lucernam rogantem audīvisset,   2!
Britannīs imperāvit ut facēs incenderent. Modestus, Vercobrigem
Britannōsque cōnspicātus, palluit.

'dī immortālēs!' inquit. 'abiit Nigrīna, appāruērunt Britannī!
mihi statim effugiendum est.'

Vercobrix tamen suīs imperāvit ut Modestum comprehenderent. 3(
ūnus ē Britannīs Modestō appropinquāvit ut dēligāret. fax, tamen,
quam tenēbat, tunicam Modestī forte incendit.

'ēheu!' ululāvit ille. 'ardeō! mē dēvorant flammae!'

tum ē manibus Britannōrum ēlāpsus fūgit praeceps. simulac per
aditum ērūpit, Strȳthiōnī amīcīsque occurrit. amphoram vīnī ē 35
manibus Aulī ēripuit et vīnum in tunicam fūdit.

'īnsānit Modestus!' clāmāvit Strȳthiō attonitus.

Modestus tamen, Strȳthiōnis clāmōrum neglegēns, amphoram in
aditum impulit. tum in amphoram innīxus, magnōs clāmōrēs
sustulit. 40

'subvenīte! subvenīte! Britannōs cēpī!'

statim manus mīlitum, ā Valeriō ducta, ad horrea contendit.

prōmōtus: prōmovēre *promote*
vallum *rampart*
trānscendērunt: trānscendere *climb over*
facēs: fax *torch*
rīmam: rīma *crack, chink*
prōspiciēbat: prōspicere *look out*
versus *having turned*

obviam iit: obviam īre *meet, go to meet*
incurrit: incurrere *bump into*
suīs: suī *his men*
ēripuit: ēripere *snatch, tear*
innīxus *having leant*
subvenīte: subvenīre *help, come to help*

tantī erant clāmōrēs Modestī ut tōta castra complērent. praefectus castrōrum ipse accurrit ut causam strepitūs cognōsceret.

Modestus exsultāns 'īnsidiās Britannīs parāvī', inquit. 4 'Vercobrix ipse multīs cum Britannīs sub horreō inclūsus est.'

breve erat certāmen. tantus erat numerus mīlitum Rōmānōrum ut Britannōs facile superārent. Rōmānī Britannōs ex horreō extractōs ad carcerem redūxērunt. tum lēgātus legiōnis ipse Modestum arcessītum laudāvit. 5

'Modeste', inquit, 'mīlitem fortiōrem quam tē numquam anteā vīdī. sōlus decem hostibus īnsidiās parāvistī. nōs decet praemium tibi dare.'

Modestus, ā lēgātō ita laudātus, adeō gaudēbat ut vix sē continēre posset. pecūniam laetus exspectābat. 5

'carcerī tē praeficiō', inquit lēgātus.

praefectus *commander*
causam: causa *reason, cause*
strepitūs: strepitus *noise, din*
breve: brevis *short, brief*

certāmen *struggle, fight*
redūxērunt: redūcere *lead back*
nōs decet *it is proper for us*
continēre *contain*

Antefix bearing name and emblem of the Twentieth Legion who were stationed at Chester after A.D.87

About the language

1 In Stage 11, you met the verb 'placet'. Notice again how it is used:

mihi placet hoc dōnum accipere.
It pleases me to receive this present.
   or, in more natural English:
I am glad to receive this present.

nōbīs placet.
It pleases us.
   or, in more natural English:
We like it.

2 The following verbs are used in a similar way:

nōs **decet** praemium Modestō dare.
It is proper for us to give a reward to Modestus.
   or, more naturally:
We ought to give a reward to Modestus.

mē **taedet** huius vītae.
It makes me tired of this life.
   or, more naturally:
I am tired of this life.

Rōmānōs numquam **oportet** hostibus crēdere.
It is never right for Romans to trust the enemy.
   or, more naturally:
Romans must never trust the enemy.

3 These verbs are known as *impersonal* verbs.

4 Further examples:

  1 tibi placet?
  2 saltātrīcem spectāre volō! mē taedet cibī et vīnī!
  3 semper pluit!
  4 Britannōs decet extrā aulam manēre.
  5 nunc advesperāscit.
  6 nōs oportet rēgnum Cogidubnī occupāre.

Practising the language

1 Study the form and meaning of the following adjectives and nouns, and give the meaning of the untranslated words:

altus	high, deep	altitūdō	height, depth
magnus	big	magnitūdō	size
pulcher	beautiful	pulchritūdō	
sollicitus		sollicitūdō	
lātus	wide	lātitūdō	
mānsuētus	tame	mānsuētūdō	
sōlus		sōlitūdō	

Give the meaning of the following nouns:

fortitūdō, longitūdō, multitūdō

Notice some slightly different examples:

cupere	to desire	cupīdō	a desire
		Cupīdō	god of Love, god of Desir
valēre	to be well	valētūdō	health: (1) good health
			(2) bad health, illness

The imperative of 'valēre' has a special meaning which you have often met:

valē   be well, i.e. fare well, goodbye

2 Complete each sentence with the right word from the list below and then translate.

missōs, līberātī, territa, regressam, tenentēs, passus

1 captīvī, ē cellīs subitō . . . . ., ad portam carceris ruērunt.
2 Britannī, hastās in manibus . . . . ., in īnsidiīs latēbant.
3 ancilla, ā dominō īrātō . . . . ., respondēre nōn audēbat.
4 Cogidubnus, tot iniūriās . . . . ., omnēs Rōmānōs ōdit.
5 māter puellam, ē tabernā tandem . . . . ., vehementer vituperāvit.
6 centuriō mīlitēs, ex Ītaliā nūper ab imperātōre . . . . ., īnspexit.

3 Translate the following sentences, then change the words in heavy print from singular to plural, and translate again. You will sometimes need to look up the gender of a noun in the 'Words and phrases' part of the Language Information section, and you may need to refer to the table of nouns on pages 160–62, especially to check the endings of *neuter* nouns.

1 imperātor **īnsulam** vīsitābat.
2 **nauta** pecūniam **poscēbat**.
3 iuvenēs **captīvum** custōdiēbant.
4 fūr **pōculum** īnspiciēbat.
5 ōmina **haruspicem** terrēbant.
6 **plaustrum** in agrō **stābat**.

4 With the help of the table of nouns on pages 160–62 in the Language Information section, complete the sentences of this exercise with the right form of each unfinished word, and then translate.

1 servus prope iānuam stābat. serv. . . pecūniam dedimus.
2 puerī per viam currēbant. clāmōrēs puer. . . mē excitāvērunt.
3 puella tabernam meam intrāvit. puell. . . multās gemmās ostendī.
4 Salvius ad aulam rēg. . . quam celerrimē contendit.
5 Memor, ubi nōm. . . tuum audīvit, perterritus erat.
6 in hāc viā sunt duo templ. . . .
7 mercātor ad fundum meum herī vēnit. frūmentum meum mercātōr. . . vēndidī.
8 magna multitūdō cīv. . . nōbīs obstābat.
9 barbarī prōvinciam oppugnāvērunt, multāsque urb. . . dēlēvērunt.
10 leōnēs saeviēbant; nam servus stultus nūllum cibum leō. . . dederat.
11 serv. . . dēnāriōs quōs tenēbam rapuērunt.
12 iūdex mercātōr. . ., quī fēminam dēcēperat, pūnīvit.

About the language

1 Study the following examples:

tanta erat multitūdō **ut tōtam aulam complēret**.
So great was the crowd that it filled the whole palace.

iuvenis gemmās adeō cupiēbat **ut pecūniam statim trāderet**.
The young man wanted the jewels so much that he handed over
the money immediately.

The groups of words in heavy print are known as *result clauses,*
because they indicate a *result*. For instance, in the first example
above, the group of words 'ut tōtam aulam complēret' indicates
the result of the crowd's size. The verb in a result clause in Latin
is always subjunctive.

2 Further examples:

1 tam stultus erat puer ut omnēs eum dērīdērent.
2 tantus erat clāmor ut nēmō iussa centuriōnum audīret.
3 Agricola tot mīlitēs ēmīsit ut hostēs fugerent.
4 adeō saeviēbat Valerius ut sē continēre nōn posset.

The legionary fortress

If the legion itself was like an army in miniature, the fortress in
which it lived when not on campaign may be compared to a fortified
town. It covered about 20–25 hectares (50–60 acres), about one
third of the area of Pompeii. The design of the fortress was based on
a standard pattern, illustrated opposite.

The chief buildings, grouped in the centre, were the headquarters
(prīncipia), the living-quarters of the commanding officer
(praetōrium), the hospital (valētūdinārium), and the granaries
(horrea). Numerous streets and alleys criss-crossed the fortress, but
there were three main streets: the 'via praetōria' ran from the main
gate to the front entrance of the principia; the 'via prīncipālis'

extended across the whole width of the fortress, making a T-junction with the via praetoria just in front of the principia; the 'via quīntāna' passed behind the principia and extended across the width of the fortress. The fortress was surrounded by a ditch, rampart and battlements, with towers at the corners and at intervals along the sides. Each side had a fortified gateway.

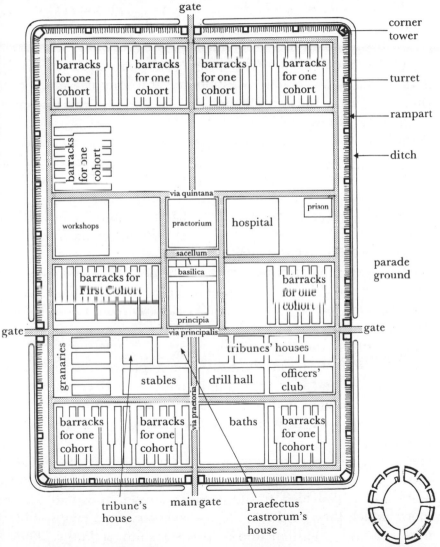

Plan of a legionary fortress (based on Chester)

amphitheatre

The principia was the heart of the legion and was therefore a large, complex and impressive building. A visitor would first enter a stone-flagged courtyard surrounded on three sides by a colonnade and storerooms. On the far side of the courtyard was the great hall or basilica, where the commander worked with his officers, interviewed important local people and administered military justice. It was a surprisingly large hall and would have looked rather like the interior of a Norman cathedral. The one at Chester, for example, was about 73 metres (240 feet) long; its central nave, bounded by tall columns supporting a vaulted roof, was 12 metres (40 feet) wide and flanked by two aisles each of 6 metres (20 feet). If each man had stood shoulder to shoulder, it would just have been possible to squeeze the entire legion into it. Whether this was ever done we do not know.

In the centre of the far long wall of the basilica and directly facing the main gate was the most sacred place in the fortress, the 'sacellum' or chapel. This housed the standard of the legion, the 'aquila', an image of an eagle perched with outspread wings on the top of a pole. It was made of gold and in its talons it clutched a bundle of golden darts that represented the thunderbolts of Jupiter. The aquila represented 'the spirit of the legion' and aroused feelings of intense loyalty and an almost religious respect. To lose it in battle was the worst possible disgrace and misfortune; it rarely happened. The soldier who looked after the aquila and carried it in battle (see the picture on p.75) was called the 'aquilifer' (eagle-bearer). He was always a soldier of the first cohort.

On either side of the sacellum were the rooms where the clerks kept the payrolls and attended to all the paperwork that was needed to run a large unit. Close by and usually underground was the legion's strong-room, in which pay and savings were kept under lock and key.

The praetorium was situated by the side of or just behind the principia. It was a fine house in the style of an Italian 'domus urbāna' and it provided the legatus and his family with those comforts which they would regard as necessary for a civilised life: central heating, a garden and a private suite of baths. These luxuries were provided for the legatus, partly because he was the commander and partly because he was a member of the highest social class and would therefore expect it. But there was probably another reason, namely to demonstrate the attractions of Roman civilisation to local civilian leaders, who were no doubt entertained in the praetorium from time to time. However, whether this display of wealth made them any happier about the taxes which they had to pay to the Romans is another question.

The valetudinarium or hospital contained many small wards for the sick and injured. There was also a large reception hall and a small operating theatre equipped with running water.

Model of stone granaries

The horrea were skilfully designed to keep grain dry and cool for long periods. In the first century A.D., like many other buildings in the fortress, they were built mainly of wood, but from the second century stone was the regular material. A granary was a long and narrow building; the roof had wide overhanging eaves to carry the rain-water away from the walls; and to prevent damp rising from the ground the floor was supported on small piers or low walls which allowed air to circulate freely underneath. There were several of these granaries in a fortress, often arranged side by side in pairs, and they could contain stocks of grain sufficient at least for one year and possibly two.

Clearly the barrack blocks, housing 5,000–6,000 men, occupied the largest area. They too were long and narrow; and they were divided into pairs of rooms, each pair providing accommodation for an eight-man section (contubernium). Along the front of the block ran a colonnaded verandah. Each section cooked for itself on a hearth in the front living-room, which was slightly the smaller of the two rooms, and slept in the larger room at the back. Each block housed a century (80 men). At the end of the block a larger suite of rooms was provided for the centurion, who may have shared it with his optio. The blocks themselves were arranged in pairs facing each other across an alley-way, as in the diagram below.

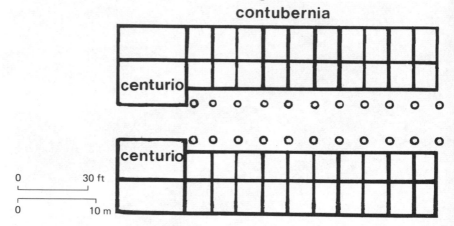

The bathhouse was regarded as an important part of military hygiene; every fortress and many smaller forts had one. Like the civilian baths, it consisted of a tepidarium, caldarium and frigidarium and served as a social club. Sometimes the military baths were outside the fortress, by a nearby stream or river, sometimes inside.

One other building, always outside, should be mentioned: the amphitheatre. It had the same shape and layout as the civilian amphitheatre and could seat the whole legion. It was used for ceremonial parades, weapon training and displays of tactics, as well as for occasional gladiatorial shows.

Not surprisingly, civilians also tended to gather round military bases. At first they were traders who set up little bars to sell appetising food and drink to supplement the plain rations served in the barracks. Naturally, too, these bars gave soldiers opportunities to meet the local girls. Legally soldiers were not allowed to marry, but the army tolerated unofficial unions. While the father lived in barracks his family grew up just outside; and his sons when they were eighteen or nineteen often followed his profession and enlisted. Many such settlements (vīcī) developed gradually into towns. A few became large, self-governing cities, such as Eboracum (York). Thus the military fortress, which had begun as a means of holding down newly conquered territory, ended by playing an important part in the development of civilian town life.

Words and phrases checklist

adeō – so much, so greatly
aditus, aditūs – entrance
adventus, adventūs – arrival
anteā – before
appāreō, appārēre, appāruī – appear
ardeō, ardēre, arsī – burn, be on fire
certāmen, certāminis – struggle, fight
comes, comitis – comrade, companion
decet – it is proper
   mē decet – I ought
fax, facis – torch
gaudeō, gaudēre – be pleased, rejoice
ignārus, ignāra, ignārum – not knowing, unaware
imperō, imperāre, imperāvī – order, command
incendō, incendere, incendī, incēnsus – burn, set fire to
īnsidiae, īnsidiārum – trap, ambush
iocus, iocī – joke
iussum, iussī – order
manus, manūs – band (of men)
noceō, nocēre, nocuī – hurt
occurrō, occurrere, occurrī – meet
ōsculum, ōsculī – kiss
praeceps, *gen.* praecipitis – headlong
praemium, praemiī – prize, reward
proximus, proxima, proximum – nearest
quālis, quāle – what sort of
silentium, silentiī – silence
sub – under, beneath
tacitus, tacita, tacitum – silent
taedet – it is tiring
   mē taedet – I am tired, I am bored
tantus, tanta, tantum – so great, such a great

imperium

post mortem Cogidubnī, Salvius rēgnum eius occupāvit. pecūniam
ā Britannīs extorquēre statim coepit. Salvium adiuvābat Belimicus,
prīnceps Canticōrum.

   prope aulam habitābat agricola Britannicus, quī Salviō
pecūniam trādere nōluit. Salvius igitur mīlitibus imperāvit ut
casam agricolae dīriperent. centuriōnem mīlitibus praefēcit.

mīlitēs, gladiīs hastīsque
armātī, casam agricolae
oppugnāvērunt.

agricola, gladiō centuriōnis
vulnerātus, exanimātus
dēcidit.

servī, clāmōribus territī,
fūgērunt.

fīlius agricolae, fūste armātus,
frūstrā restitit.

Belimicus, spē praemiī
adductus, mīlitēs Rōmānōs
adiuvābat et incitābat.

mīlitēs casam intrāvērunt et
arcam, pecūniā complētam,
extulērunt.

deinde mīlitēs fēminās, catēnīs vīnctās, abdūxērunt.

postrēmō mīlitēs casam incendērunt. flammae, ventō auctae, casam celeriter cōnsūmpsērunt.

pāstōrēs, quī prope casam habitābant, immōtī stābant, spectāculō attonitī.

casam vīdērunt, flammīs cōnsūmptam.

fīlium agricolae vīdērunt, hastā graviter vulnerātum.

agricolam ipsum vīdērunt, gladiō centuriōnis interfectum.

tandem abiērunt, timōre īrāque commōtī, Belimicum Rōmānōsque vituperantēs.

testāmentum

ego, Tiberius Claudius Cogidubnus, rēx magnus Britannōrum, morbō gravī afflīctus, hoc testāmentum fēcī.

ego Titum Flāvium Domitiānum, optimum Imperātōrum, hērēdem meum faciō. mandō T. Flāviō Domitiānō rēgnum meum cīvēsque Rēgnēnsēs. iubeō cīvēs Rēgnēnsēs lēgibus pārēre et vītam 5 quiētam agere. nam prīncipēs Rēgnēnsium mē saepe vexāvērunt. aliī, spē praedae adductī, inter sē pugnāvērunt; aliī, īnsāniā affectī, sēditiōnem contrā Rōmānōs facere temptāvērunt. nunc tamen eōs omnēs oportet discordiam huius modī dēpōnere.

dō lēgō Cn. Iūliō Agricolae statuam meam, ā fabrō Britannicō 10 factam. sīc Agricola mē per tōtam vītam in memoriā habēre potest.

dō lēgō C. Salviō Līberālī, fidēlissimo amīcōrum meōrum, duōs tripodas argenteōs. Salvius vir summae prūdentiae est.

dō lēgō L. Marciō Memorī vīllam meam prope Aquās Sūlis sitam. L. Marcius Memor, ubi aeger ad thermās vēnī, ut auxilium ā deā 15 Sūle peterem, benignē mē excēpit.

dō lēgō Dumnorigī, prīncipī Rēgnēnsium, quem sīcut fīlium dīlēxī, mīlle aureōs aulamque meam, sī forte Dumnorix mortuus est, haec C. Salviō Līberālī lēgō.

dō lēgō Belimicō, prīncipī Canticōrum, quīngentōs aureōs et 20 nāvem celerrimam. Belimicus enim mē ab ursā ōlim servāvit, quae per aulam meam saeviēbat.

mandō C. Salviō Līberālī cūram fūneris meī. volō Salvium corpus meum sepelīre. volō eum mēcum sepelīre gemmās meās, paterās aureās, omnia arma quae ad bellum vēnātiōnemque comparāvī. 25

mandō C. Salviō Līberālī hoc testāmentum, manū meā scrīptum ānulōque meō signātum. dolus malus ab hōc testāmentō abestō!

lēgibus: lēx *law*	mīlle *a thousand*
praedae: praeda *booty, plunder*	celerrimam: celer *quick, fast*
adductī: addūcere *lead on, encourage*	corpus *body*
affectī: afficere *affect*	sepelīre *bury*
discordiam: discordia *strife*	dolus . . . abestō! *may . . .*
in memoriā habēre *keep in mind, remember*	*trickery keep away!*
benignē *kindly*	malus *evil, bad*
excēpit: excipere *receive*	

When you have read each section, answer the questions that follow it.

in aulā Salviī

I

Salvius, cum dē morte Cogidubnī audīvisset, ē castrīs discessit. per prōvinciam iter fēcit ad aulam quam ē testāmentō accēperat. ibi novem diēs manēbat ut rēs Cogidubnī administrāret. decimō diē, iterum profectus, pecūniās opēsque ā Britannīs extorquēre incēpit. plūrimī prīncipēs, avāritiā et metū corruptī, Salvium adiuvābant. 5

Belimicus, prīnceps Canticōrum, spē praemiī adductus, Salviō summum auxilium dedit. Britannōs omnia bona trādere coēgit. aliī, quī potentiam Salviī timēbant, Belimicō statim cessērunt; aliī, quī eī resistēbant, poenās gravēs dedērunt.

Belimicus autem, quamquam prō hōc auxiliō multa praemia 1 honōrēsque ā Salviō accēpit, haudquāquam contentus erat. rēx enim Rēgnēnsium esse cupiēbat. hāc spē adductus, cum paucīs prīncipibus coniūrāre coepit. quī tamen, Belimicō diffīsī, rem Salviō rettulērunt.

Salvius, audāciā Belimicī incēnsus, eum interficere cōnstituit. 1 amīcōs igitur, quibus maximē cōnfīdēbat, ad sē vocāvit; eōs in aulam ingressōs rogāvit utrum vim an venēnum adhibēret. amīcī, ut favōrem Salviī conciliārent, multa et varia cōnsilia prōposuērunt.

tandem ūnus ex amīcīs, vir callidissimus, 'venēnum', inquit, 'Belimicō, hostī īnfestō, aptissimum est.' 2

'sed quō modō tālem rem efficere possumus?' inquit Salvius. 'nam Belimicus, vir magnae prūdentiae, nēminī cōnfīdit.'

'hunc homunculum dēcipere nōbīs facile est', inquit ille. 'venēnum cibō mixtum multōs virōs callidiōrēs quam Belimicum iam fefellit. ipse sciō venēnum perītē dare.' 2

'euge!' inquit Salvius, cōnsiliō amīcī dēlectātus. 'facillimum est mihi illum ad cēnam sūmptuōsam invītāre. mē oportet epistulam blandam eī mittere. verbīs enim mollibus ac blandīs resistere nōn potest.'

Salvius igitur Belimicum ad aulam sine morā invītāvit. quī, 30 epistulā mendācī dēceptus neque ūllam fraudem suspicātus, ad aulam nōnā hōrā vēnit.

decimō: decimus *tenth*	īnfestō: īnfestus *dangerous*
profectus *having set out*	aptissimum: aptus *suitable*
avāritiā: avāritia *greed*	mixtum: miscēre *mix*
metū: metus *fear*	fefellit: fallere *deceive*
prō *for, in return for*	sūmptuōsam: sūmptuōsus *expensive, lavish*
bona *goods*	blandam: blandus *flattering*
haudquāquam *not at all*	mollibus: mollis *soft*
rettulērunt: referre *tell, report*	morā: mora *delay*
audāciā: audācia *boldness, audacity*	neque *and not*
incēnsus *inflamed, angered*	ūllam: ūllus *any*
utrum . . . an *whether . . . or*	fraudem: fraus *trick*
favōrem: favor *favour*	nōnā: nōnus *ninth*
conciliārent: conciliāre *win, gain*	

1 Where does Salvius travel to when he hears of Cogidubnus' death?
2 How long does Salvius stay there? Why?
3 What does Salvius do next? How does Belimicus help him?
4 Why does Belimicus stop helping Salvius and start plotting?
5 How does Salvius find out about Delimicus' plot?
6 What decision does Salvius take when he hears of Belimicus' treachery? What question does he put to his friends?
7 Which suggestion does Salvius accept? What are the advantages of this method?
8 How does he lure Belimicus into his trap?

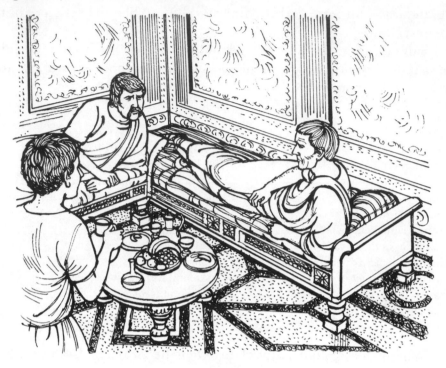

II

Belimicum aulam intrantem Salvius benignē excēpit et in triclīnium
addūxit. ibi sōlī sūmptuōsē atque hilarē cēnābant. Belimicus,
Salvium rīdentem cōnspicātus vīnōque solūtus, audācter dīcere
coepit.

'mī Salvī, multa et magna beneficia ā mē accēpistī. postquam 5
effūgērunt Quīntus et Dumnorix, ego sōlus tē adiūvī; multōs
continuōs diēs eōs persecūtus Dumnorigem occīdī; multa falsa
Agricolae dīxī ut Cogidubnum perfidiae damnārem; post mortem
eius, Britannōs pecūniam bonaque sua trādere coēgī. prō hīs tantīs
beneficiīs praemium meritum rogō.'   1

Salvius, ubi haec audīvit, arrogantiā Belimicī incēnsus, īram
tamen cēlāvit et cōmiter respondit.

'praemium meritum iam tibi parāvī. sed cūr nihil cōnsūmis, mī
amīce? volō tē garum exquīsitissimum gustāre quod ex Hispāniā
importāvī. puer! fer mihi et Belimicō illud garum!'   1

cum servus garum ambōbus dedisset, Salvius ad hospitem versus,

'dīc mihi, Belimice', inquit, 'quid prō hīs tantīs beneficiīs repetis?'

'iam ex testāmentō Cogidubnī', respondit ille, 'quīngentōs aureōs accēpī. id haudquāquam satis est. rēgnum ipsum repetō.'   20

quod cum audīvisset, Salvius 'ego', inquit, 'nōn Cogidubnus, aureōs tibi dedī. cūr haud satis est?'

'quid dīcis?' exclāmāvit Belimicus. 'hoc nōn intellegō.'

'illud testāmentum', respondit Salvius, 'est falsum. nōn Cogidubnus sed ego scrīpsī.'   25

addūxit: addūcere *lead*
sūmptuōsē *lavishly*
atque *and*
hilarē *in high spirits, merrily*
vīnō . . . solūtus *relaxed by the wine*
persecūtus *having pursued*
damnārem: damnāre *condemn*
meritum: meritus *well-deserved*
Hispāniā: Hispānia *Spain*
repetis: repetere *claim*
haud *not*

1 How is Belimicus received and treated when he comes to the palace?
2 What makes Salvius angry (line 11)? Why do you think he hides his anger?
3 What does Belimicus think Salvius means by a 'praemium meritum' (line 13)? What does Salvius really mean?
4 During the meal, Belimicus changes his tactics: instead of continuing with his plot, he asks Salvius directly for the kingship. What has encouraged him to do this?
5 What has Belimicus already received? How? What does he now learn about the will?

About the language

1 Study the following sentences:

iuvenis, **gladiō** armātus, ad castra contendit.
The young man, armed with a sword, hurried to the camp.

Britannī, **tantā iniūriā** incēnsī, sēditiōnem fēcērunt.
The Britons, angered by such great injustice, revolted.

mīles, **vulnere** impedītus, tandem cessit.
The soldier, hindered by his wound, gave in at last.

senex, **multīs cūrīs** vexātus, dormīre nōn poterat.
The old man, troubled by many cares, was unable to sleep.

cīvēs, **clāmōribus** excitātī, ē lectīs surrēxērunt.
The citizens, awakened by the shouts, rose from their beds.

The words in heavy print are in the *ablative* case.

2 Compare the nominative singular with the ablative singular and ablative plural in the first, second and third declensions:

	nominative singular	*ablative singular*	*ablative plural*
1st declension	puella	puellā	puellīs
2nd declension	servus	servō	servīs
	puer	puerō	puerīs
	templum	templō	templīs
3rd declension	mercātor	mercātōre	mercātōribus
	leō	leōne	leōnibus
	cīvis	cīve	cīvibus
	rēx	rēge	rēgibus
	urbs	urbe	urbibus
	nōmen	nōmine	nōminibus

3 Further examples:

1 Salvius, audāciā Belimicī attonitus, nihil dīxit.
2 mercātor, fūstibus verberātus, in fossā exanimātus iacēbat.
3 mīlitēs, vallō dēfēnsī, barbarīs diū resistēbant.
4 uxor mea ānulum, gemmīs ōrnātum, ēmit.
5 hospitēs, arte ancillae dēlectātī, plausērunt.

Belimicus rēx

Belimicus, cum haec audīvisset, adeō attonitus erat ut nihil respondēre posset. Salvius autem haec addidit rīdēns,

'mī amīce, cūr tam attonitus es? tū et Cogidubnus semper inimīcī erātis. num quicquam ab illō spērāvistī? nōs autem in amīcitiā sumus. tibi multum dēbeō, ut dīxistī. itaque rēgem tē creāre in 5 animō habeō. sed rēgnum quod tibi dēstinō multō maius est quam Cogidubnī. heus! puer! plūs garī!'

servus, cui Salvius hoc imperāvit, statim exiit. brevī regressus, garum venēnō mixtum intulit atque in Belimicī pateram effūdit. tam laetus erat ille, ubi verba Salviī audīvit, ut garum cōnsūmeret, 10 ignārus perīculī mortis.

'quantum est hoc rēgnum quod mihi prōmīsistī? ubi gentium est?' rogāvit Belimicus.

Salvius cachinnāns 'multō maius est', inquit, 'quam imperium Rōmānum.' 15

Belimicus hīs verbīs perturbātus,

'nimium bibistī, mī amīce', inquit. 'nūllum rēgnum nōvī maius quam imperium Rōmānum.'

'rēgnum est, quō omnēs tandem abeunt', respondit Salvius. 'rēgnum est, unde nēmō redīre potest. Belimice, tē rēgem creō 20 mortuōrum.'

Belimicus, metū mortis pallidus, surrēxit. haerēbat lingua in gutture; tintinnābant aurēs; ventrem, quī iam graviter dolēbat, prēnsāvit. metū īrāque commōtus exclāmāvit,

'tū mihi nocēre nōn audēs, quod omnia scelera tua Agricolae 25 dēnūntiāre possum.'

'mē dēnūntiāre nōn potes, Belimice, quod nunc tibi imminet mors. nunc tibi abeundum est in rēgnum tuum. avē atque valē, mī Belimice.'

Belimicus, venēnō excruciātus, pugiōnem tamen in Salvium 30 coniēcit, spē ultiōnis adductus. deinde magnum gemitum dedit et humī dēcidit mortuus. Salvius, pugiōne leviter vulnerātus, servō imperāvit ut medicum arcesseret. aliī servī corpus Belimicī ē triclīniō extractum quam celerrimē cremāvērunt. sīc Belimicus arrogantiae poenās dedit; sīc Salvius cēterīs prīncipibus persuāsit ut 35 in fidē manērent.

spērāvistī: spērāre *hope, expect*
creāre *make, create*
dēstinō: dēstināre *intend*
effūdit: effundere *pour out*
ubi gentium? *where in the world?*
perturbātus: perturbāre *disturb, alarm*
lingua *tongue*
gutture: guttur *throat*
tintinnābant: tintinnāre *ring*
ventrem: venter *stomach*

graviter dolēbat: graviter dolēre
  be extremely painful
scelera: scelus *crime*
dēnūntiāre *denounce, reveal*
imminet: imminēre *hang over*
tibi abeundum est *you must go away*
avē atque valē *hail and farewell*
excruciātus: excruciāre *torture, torment*
leviter *slightly*
cremāvērunt: cremāre *cremate*

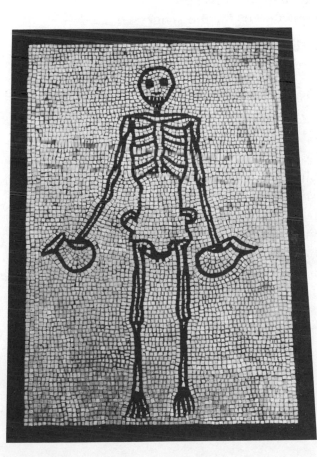

About the language

1 Study the following examples:

lēgātus sermōnem cum Quīntō **duās hōrās** habēbat.
The commander talked with Quintus for two hours.

quattuor diēs fugitīvus in silvā latēbat.
For four days, the runaway lay hidden in the wood.

In each of these sentences, the words in heavy print indicate *how
long* something went on; for this, Latin uses the *accusative* case.

2 Now study the following:

tertiā hōrā nūntiī advēnērunt.
At the third hour, the messengers arrived.

quīntō diē Agricola pugnāre cōnstituit.
On the fifth day, Agricola decided to fight.

In these sentences, the words in heavy print indicate *when*
something happened; for this, Latin uses the *ablative* case.

3 Further examples:

1 hospitēs trēs hōrās cēnābant.
2 quārtō diē revēnit rēx.
3 Agricola prōvinciam septem annōs administrāvit.
4 secundā hōrā lībertus Memorem excitāre temptāvit.
5 mediā nocte hostēs castra nostra oppugnāvērunt.
6 sex diēs nāvigābāmus; septimō diē ad portum advēnimus.

Practising the language

1 Study the form and meaning of the following adjectives and nouns, and give the meaning of the untranslated words:

avārus	greedy, miserly	avāritia	greed
amīcus	friendly	amīcitia	friendship
superbus	proud	superbia	
trīstis		trīstitia	
perītus		perītia	skill, experience
sapiēns		sapientia	
prūdēns		prūdentia	sense
perfidus	treacherous, untrustworthy	perfidia	
ēlegāns	elegant, tasteful	ēlegantia	
benevolēns	kind	benevolentia	

Give the meaning of the following nouns:

laetitia, audācia, arrogantia, īnsānia, potentia

2 Complete each of the sentences below with one of the following groups of words and then translate. Use each group of words once only.

ut nēmō centuriōnem audīret
ut Belimicum interficeret
ut ad castra redīrent
quō modō Cogidubnus periisset
cum tabernam intrāvissent

1 Salvius cibum venēnō mixtum parāvit . . . . . .
2 Quīntus nesciēbat . . . . . .
3 cīvēs, ..., vīnum poposcērunt.
4 tantus erat clāmor . . . . . .
5 Agricola mīlitibus imperāvit . . . . . .

3 Complete each sentence with the most suitable word from the list below, and then translate.

audāciā, vīnō, gladiō, īrā, catēnīs

1 nūntius, ... graviter vulnerātus, effugere nōn poterat.
2 Salvius, ... eius attonitus, diū tacēbat.
3 captīvī, ... vīnctī, in longīs ōrdinibus stābant.
4 dominus, ... commōtus, omnēs servōs carnificibus trādidit.
5 hospitēs, ... solūtī, clāmāre et iocōs facere coepērunt.

About the language

1 From Stage 1 onwards, you have met phrases of the following kind:

ad fundum   to the farm
ex ātriō   out of the hall
per viās   through the streets
cum amīcīs   with friends

The words in heavy print are *prepositions*. A preposition is normally used with a noun in the accusative or ablative case.

2 The prepositions 'ad', 'per' and 'prope' are used with the *accusative*:

ad **rēgem**   to the king
per **flammās**   through the flames
prope **sellam**   near the chair

Other prepositions used with the accusative are 'ante', 'circum', 'contrā', 'extrā', 'inter', 'post' and 'trāns'.

3 The prepositions 'ā', 'ab', 'cum', 'ē' and 'ex' are used with the *ablative*:

ab **amphitheātrō**   from the amphitheatre
ex **oppidō**   out of the town
cum **hospitibus**   with the guests

Other prepositions used with the ablative are 'dē', 'prō' and 'sine'.

4 Notice how the preposition 'in' is used:

cīvēs **in forum** cucurrērunt.   The citizens ran into the forum.
mercātōrēs **in forō** negōtium   The merchants were doing
agēbant.   business in the forum.

ancilla centuriōnem   The slave-girl led the centurion
in tabernam dūxit.   into the inn.
canis **in tabernā** dormiēbat.   The dog was sleeping in the inn.

'in' meaning '*into*' is used with the accusative.
'in' meaning '*in*' is used with the ablative.

5 Further examples:

1 duo amīcī ad urbem iter faciēbant.
2 prope templum deae erat fōns sacer.
3 prīncipēs dē morte Belimicī sermōnem habēbant.
4 prō aulā stābant quattuor custōdēs.
5 mīlitēs in castrīs labōrābant.
6 Agricola in castra contendit.
7 centuriō sine mīlitibus revēnit.
8 gubernātor nāvem circum saxum dīrēxit.

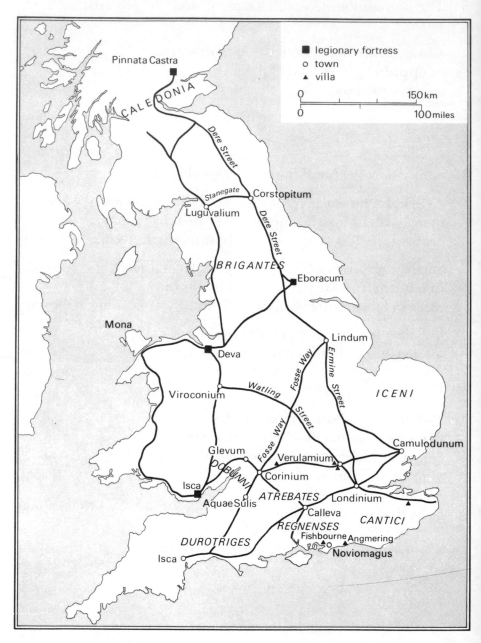

Britain in the first century A.D.

Interpreting the evidence : our knowledge of Roman Britain

Our knowledge of the Roman occupation of Britain is based on three types of evidence:
(1) *literary* evidence, what the Romans wrote about Britain;
(2) *archaeological* evidence: what archaeologists have discovered during excavations, including:
(3) *inscriptional* evidence: inscriptions in Latin (and sometimes Greek) from tombstones, altars, public buildings and monuments, and from private objects such as writing-tablets, defixiones etc.

All of this material has to be interpreted before we can begin to understand it. The writings have to be translated and the exact meanings of technical terms have to be found; discoveries made on an archaeological site have to be noted down and different periods identified so that remains can be dated; inscriptions have to be deciphered, translated and, where possible, dated. It is a long and complicated process, in which one type of evidence can often help us to understand another type. To see how it works in practice, we shall examine examples from each type of evidence.

Literary evidence

There are two well-known Latin writings about Roman Britain. One is Julius Caesar's account in which he describes his brief reconnaissance mission to the Kent coast in 55 B.C. and his return in greater force the following year when he stormed the fortress of a British king before withdrawing again. The other is Tacitus' account of the life of his father-in-law, Agricola. More than half of this is devoted to Agricola's governorship of Britain, including such exploits as the circumnavigation of Britain and the defeat of the Scots in the great battle of Mons Graupius.

Both pieces of writing are to some extent biased. Caesar wrote his account in order to justify his actions to the Senate in Rome and place himself in a favourable light; Tacitus was anxious to preserve the memory of his father-in-law and to praise his success as governor.

In chapter 21 of his biography, Tacitus tells us that under Agricola an extensive programme of romanisation was carried out, including the building of 'fora' or town centres in some of the larger and well-established settlements in the south-east of Britain. This was confirmed by the discovery, during an excavation, of fragments of an inscription which was designed to stand over the entrance to the new forum at Verulamium (St Albans). It mentions the name of Agricola in connection with the building of the forum. (A reproduction of the inscription appears on p. 108.)

Tacitus also tells us of Roman plans to improve the education of the British:

> 'Agricola arranged for the sons of British chiefs to receive a broad education. He made it clear that he preferred the natural abilities of the British to the skill and training of the Gauls. As a result, instead of hating the language of the Romans, they became very keen to learn it.'

This may sound as if Tacitus is exaggerating. However, we know from inscriptions that Salvius, who was a distinguished lawyer, was sent to Britain at about this time, and one of his tasks may have been to help the British bring their laws into line with Roman law. If this was so, there may be a link between Salvius' presence in Britain and Tacitus' statement that the British were eager to learn Latin; they may have wished not only to have conversations with the occupying forces, but also to understand the complexities of Roman law.

Archaeological evidence

The task of an archaeologist is to uncover and to help us understand the remains of the past. To do this he or she must first decide on a suitable site to excavate. Some sites are already well-known but have not been completely excavated; sometimes sites are found by accident. A workman digging a drain across a field in 1962 hit fragments of a mosaic floor and this chance discovery led to the excavation of the palace at Fishbourne. Building and road works can often uncover evidence of a site. In such cases archaeologists may have a very limited time in which to excavate before the bulldozers move in and destroy the evidence for ever.

Once the site has been located, the archaeologist has to plan and carry out a careful excavation of the area. This means uncovering the foundations of buildings, mosaic floors and other large structures, and carefully sifting the soil for pieces of pottery, items of jewellery, coins and other small objects. However, the purpose of an excavation is not simply to find precious objects but to discover as much as possible about the people who used the buildings, what their life was like, when they lived there and even perhaps what happened to them. In order to do this an archaeologist must be trained, rather like a detective, to observe every small detail and to piece together all the evidence that is found.

As the earth is removed from a site, the archaeologist will watch for two things: the existence and position of any wall foundations, and the way in which the various levels or layers of earth change colour and texture as the trenches are dug deeper. If one wall is built directly on top of another, it is reasonable to assume that the lower wall is from an earlier building.

Roman coins can usually be accurately dated because they have the emperors' heads and names stamped on them. If a coin of Nero is found in a layer, then the date of the layer can be no earlier than A.D. 54 since Nero was not emperor until then. If no coins of later emperors are found in the layer, then it is reasonable to assume that the layer dates from Nero's reign (A.D. 54 to 68) or from the short period afterwards during which coins of Nero's reign continued to circulate.

Fairly accurate dates are also obtainable from a study of the styles and patterns of pottery found on a site. Large quantities have survived, as pottery is a durable material which does not rot, and broken pieces (sherds) are found in very large numbers on many sites. All kinds of pottery were used throughout the Roman world and the presence on a British site of pottery which has come from Italy or Gaul shows that the owner was wealthy enough to pay for imported material. In ways such as this the archaeologist can begin to assemble information about the people who occupied the site.

Layers of ash, charred pottery and other burnt objects will indicate a destruction by fire; a mass of broken rubble may suggest that a building was demolished, perhaps to make way for a larger, better one. Many sites in Britain show a gradual development from a simple timber-framed farmhouse building, which was replaced by a larger stone house, to a grander, multi-roomed mansion with baths, mosaic pavements and colonnades.

By such painstaking processes archaeologists have been able to reconstruct a remarkably detailed picture of the Roman occupation of Britain. The fact that most of the Romano-British villas were sited in the south-east, whereas the military fortresses were established in the north and west, suggests that Britain at this period was largely peaceful and prosperous in the south-east but still troubled by the threat of hostile tribes in the north-west. Traces of a vast network of Roman roads have been found, showing just how numerous and effective communications must have been. Parts of many Romano-British towns have been excavated, revealing how advanced urban life was. It is not uncommon to find the remains of an extensive forum, carefully laid out grids of streets, the foundations of many large buildings including temples with altars and inscriptions, sometimes a theatre and an amphitheatre, and substantial city walls.

The excavation of military sites, such as forts, marching camps and legionary fortresses, has shown how important the army was in maintaining peace and protection for Roman Britain. It has also shown very clearly the movements of the legions around the country and added considerably to our knowledge of the Roman army.

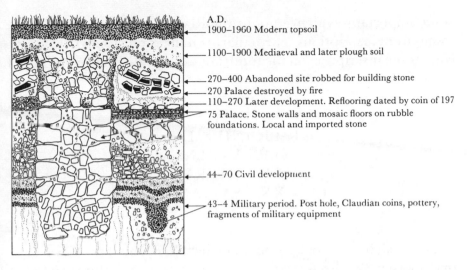

A.D.
1900–1960 Modern topsoil

1100–1900 Mediaeval and later plough soil

270–400 Abandoned site robbed for building stone
270 Palace destroyed by fire
110–270 Later development. Reflooring dated by coin of 197
75 Palace. Stone walls and mosaic floors on rubble foundations. Local and imported stone

44–70 Civil development

43–4 Military period. Post hole, Claudian coins, pottery, fragments of military equipment

Diagram showing layers of evidence for occupation at Fishbourne

Inscriptional evidence

Some important evidence about the Roman occupation of Britain comes from inscriptions, particularly on the tombstones of soldiers. Here is the inscription on the tombstone of a soldier who was buried at Chester.

D M

L LICINIUS L F

TER   VALENS

ARE VETERAN

LEG XX VV AN VL

H S E

At first sight, this looks difficult to decipher. The task, however, is made easier by the fact that most of these inscriptions follow a standard pattern. The items are usually arranged in the following order:

(1) The dedication at the top of the stone – D M – abbreviation for 'Dīs Mānibus', the spirits of the departed.

(2) The praenomen. This is first of a citizen's three names and is usually abbreviated to a single letter, as here – L for 'Lūcius'.

(3) The nomen. Always given in full, as here – 'Licinius'.

(4) The father's name. It is usually only the father's praenomen that is given, and this can be recognised in abbreviated form by the single letter which comes before an F representing 'fīlius'. The son often had the same praenomen as his father, as here – L F for 'Lūciī fīlius'.

(5) Tribe. Roman soldiers were Roman citizens and were therefore enrolled in one of the thirty-five Roman tribes. The name of the tribe is abbreviated, as here – TER for 'Teretīna'.

(6) The cognomen. This is the last of the three names, usually placed after the father's name and the Roman tribe in which the soldier was enrolled. It is always given in full, as here – 'Valēns'. Three names were a mark of Roman citizenship and therefore an important indication of status.

(7) Birthplace. This can usually be identified as a town in the Roman empire, thus ARE for 'Arelātē' (modern Arles in the south of France).

(8) Rank and legion. They are usually both abbreviated – VETERAN for 'veterānus'; LEG XX VV for 'legiōnis XX Valeriae Victrīcis'.

(9) Age. This is represented by AN or ANN for 'annōrum', followed by a number. This number is in most cases rounded off to a multiple of 5. Sometimes VIX ('vīxit' = lived) is placed before AN.

(10) Length of service (not included in the inscription above). This is represented by STIP followed by a number, e.g. STIP X for 'stipendia X' (ten years' service).

(11) The final statement. This is abbreviated, and usually takes the form of H S E for 'hīc situs est' (is buried here) or H F C for 'hērēs faciendum cūrāvit' (his heir had this stone set up).

The Chester inscription can therefore be interpreted as follows:

D(IS) M(ANIBUS)
L(UCIUS) LICINIUS L(UCII) F(ILIUS)
TER(ETINA) VALENS
ARE(LATE) VETERAN(US)
LEG(IONIS) XX V(ALERIAE) V(ICTRICIS) AN(NORUM)
V L
H(IC) S(ITUS) E(ST)

This stone is dedicated to the spirits of the departed. Lucius Licinius Valens, son of Lucius, of the Teretine tribe, from Arelate, veteran of the Twentieth Legion Valeria Victrix, aged 45, is buried here.

Here is the inscription on another soldier's tombstone, also found at Chester.

D M

CÆC ILIVS·AVIT
VS·EMER·AVG
OPTIO LEG XX
VVSTP·XV·VIX.
AN.XXXIIII
H F C

Try to find out from it the following information:

1 The soldier's name   4 His age at death
2 His rank   5 The length of his service
3 His legion

In the same way, find as much information as you can from the following inscription:

GLOVESIVS·PAPR
CADARVS·EMERTA·M
LEG·XX·V·V·AN·XX·V·ST·IIX
FRONTNVS·AQVILO·H·F·C

Words and phrases checklist

ac – and
arrogantia, arrogantiae – cheek, arrogance
atque – and
beneficium, beneficiī – act of kindness, favour
cōnstituō, cōnstituere, cōnstituī, cōnstitūtus – decide
corpus, corporis – body
dīligō, dīligere, dīlēxī, dīlēctus – be fond of
doleō, dolēre, doluī – hurt, be in pain
gemitus, gemitūs – groan
hērēs, hērēdis – heir
īra, īrae – anger
lingua, linguae – tongue
malus, mala, malum – evil, bad
mandō, mandāre, mandāvī, mandātus – entrust, hand over
metus, metūs – fear

mīlle – a thousand
    mīlia – thousands
multō – much
occīdō, occīdere, occīdī, occīsus – kill
opēs, opum – money, wealth
pallidus, pallida, pallidum – pale
praeficiō, praeficere, praefēcī, praefectus – put in charge
quicquam (*also spelt* quidquam) – anything
sīc – thus, in this way
solvō, solvere, solvī, solūtus – loosen, untie
spēs, speī – hope
suspicātus, suspicāta, suspicātum – having suspected
testāmentum, testāmentī – will
ut – as
ventus, ventī – wind

ūnus – one	vīgintī – twenty
duo – two	trīgintā – thirty
trēs – three	quadrāgintā – forty
quattuor – four	quīnquāgintā – fifty
quīnque – five	sexāgintā – sixty
sex – six	septuāgintā – seventy
septem – seven	octōgintā – eighty
octō – eight	nōnāgintā – ninety
novem – nine	centum – a hundred
decem – ten	ducentī – two hundred

Language
Information

Contents

PART ONE: About the language

Nouns

1 You have met the following cases:

	first declension	*second declension*		
	f.	*m.*	*m.*	*n.*
SINGULAR				
nominative and vocative	puella	servus (*voc.* serve)	puer	templum
accusative	puellam	servum	puerum	templum
genitive	puellae	servī	puerī	templī
dative	puellae	servō	puerō	templō
PLURAL				
nominative and vocative	puellae	servī	puerī	templa
accusative	puellās	servōs	puerōs	templa
genitive	puellārum	servōrum	puerōrum	templōrum
dative	puellīs	servīs	puerīs	templīs

Notes:

1 Notice again how the genitive and the dative cases are used:

genitive: sacerdōtēs ad aulam **rēgis** contendēbant.
The priests were hurrying to the palace of the king.

prīnceps nōmina **puellārum** nōn audīvit.
The chieftain did not hear the names of the girls.

dative: agricola **mercātōrī** fundum ostendēbat.
The farmer was showing the farm to the merchant.

caupō **puerīs** vīnum dedit.
The innkeeper gave wine to the boys.

2 The main forms of the *ablative* case are given on page 138, Stage 28.

third declension

m.	m.	m.	m.	f.	n.	
						SINGULAR
mercātor	leō	cīvis	rēx	urbs	nōmen	nominative and vocative
mercātōrem	leōnem	cīvem	rēgem	urbem	nōmen	accusative
mercātōris	leōnis	cīvis	rēgis	urbis	nōminis	genitive
mercātōrī	leōnī	cīvī	regī	urbī	nōminī	dative
						PLURAL
mercātōrēs	leōnēs	cīvēs	rēgēs	urbēs	nōmina	nominative and vocative
mercātōrēs	leōnēs	cīvēs	rēgēs	urbēs	nōmina	accusative
mercātōrum	leōnum	cīvium	rēgum	urbium	nōminum	genitive
mercātōribus	leōnibus	cīvibus	rēgibus	urbibus	nōminibus	dative

2 Translate each sentence, then change the words in heavy print from singular to plural, and translate again.

1 ancilla **cīvī** aquam obtulit.
2 latrōnēs **nūntium rēgis** interfēcērunt.
3 amīcus noster **nāvem mercātōris** vīdit.
4 māter **stolam puellae** laudāvit.

3 Translate each sentence, then change the words in heavy print from plural to singular, and translate again.

1 senex **puellīs** pecūniam reddidit.
2 imperātor **uxōrēs cīvium** ad aulam vocāvit.
3 sacerdōtēs **iānuās templōrum** aperuērunt.
4 medicus **oculōs mīlitum** īnspexit.

4 Study the following nouns:

	fourth declension		fifth declension
	f.	n.	m.
SINGULAR			
nominative and vocative	manus	genū	diēs
accusative	manum	genū	diem
genitive	manūs	genūs	diēī
dative	manuī	genū	diēī
PLURAL			
nominative and vocative	manūs	genua	diēs
accusative	manūs	genua	diēs
genitive	manuum	genuum	diērum
dative	manibus	genibus	diēbus

'manus' and 'genū' belong to the *fourth* declension, and 'diēs' to the *fifth*. Compare their endings with those of the other declensions. Notice especially the form and pronunciation of the genitive singular, nominative plural and accusative plural of 'manus'.

5 With the help of paragraph 4, find the Latin for the words in italics in the following sentences:

1 Seven *days* had now passed.
2 The priest raised his *hand*.
3 The injured man's *knees* were very painful.
4 The mother washed the child's *hands* and face.
5 It was the sixth hour of the *day*.

Adjectives

1 The following adjectives belong to the 1st and 2nd declension:

	masculine	*feminine*	*neuter*	*masculine*	*feminine*	*neuter*
SINGULAR						
nominative and vocative	bonus (*voc.* bone)	bona	bonum	pulcher	pulchra	pulchrum
accusative	bonum	bonam	bonum	pulchrum	pulchram	pulchrum
genitive	bonī	bonae	bonī	pulchrī	pulchrae	pulchrī
dative	bonō	bonae	bonō	pulchrō	pulchrae	pulchrō
PLURAL						
nominative and vocative	bonī	bonae	bona	pulchrī	pulchrae	pulchra
accusative	bonōs	bonās	bona	pulchrōs	pulchrās	pulchra
genitive	bonōrum	bonārum	bonōrum	pulchrōrum	pulchrārum	pulchrōrum
dative		bonīs			pulchrīs	

2 The following adjectives belong to the 3rd declension:

	masc. and fem.	*neuter*	*masc. and fem.*	*neuter*
SINGULAR				
nominative and vocative	fortis	forte	ingēns	ingēns
accusative	fortem	forte	ingentem	ingēns
genitive	fortis		ingentis	
dative	fortī		ingentī	
PLURAL				
nominative and vocative	fortēs	fortia	ingentēs	ingentia
accusative	fortēs	fortia	ingentēs	ingentia
genitive	fortium		ingentium	
dative	fortibus		ingentibus	

3 Using paragraphs 1 and 2 and the gender information in the table of nouns on pages 4 and 5, find the Latin for the words in italics in the following sentences:

1 The *beautiful* temple stood in the middle of the city.
2 This is the house of a *brave* citizen.
3 The craftsmen built three *huge* temples.
4 They set up a statue to the *good* girl.

Comparison of adjectives (i.e. comparative and superlative forms)

1 You have met the following comparative and superlative forms
of the adjective:

	comparative	*superlative*
longus	longior	longissimus
long	*longer*	*very long*
pulcher	pulchrior	pulcherrimus
beautiful	*more beautiful*	*very beautiful*
fortis	fortior	fortissimus
brave	*braver*	*very brave*
fēlīx	fēlīcior	fēlīcissimus
lucky	*luckier*	*very lucky*
prūdēns	prūdentior	prūdentissimus
shrewd	*shrewder*	*very shrewd*

Notice the following example:

facilis	facilior	facillimus
easy	*easier*	*very easy*

2 Irregular forms:

bonus	melior	optimus
good	*better*	*very good, best*
malus	peior	pessimus
bad	*worse*	*very bad, worst*
magnus	maior	maximus
big	*bigger*	*very big*
parvus	minor	minimus
small	*smaller*	*very small*
multus	plūs	plūrimus
much	*more*	*very much*

which becomes in the plural:

multī	plūrēs	plūrimī
many	*more*	*very many, most*

3   Translate the following examples:

1 'nēmō fortior est quam Modestus', inquit Vilbia.
2 longissima erat pompa, pulcherrima quoque.
3 peior es quam fūr!
4 Salviī vīlla erat minor quam aula Cogidubnī.
5 facillimum erat nōbīs urbem capere.
6 numquam tabernam meliōrem quam tuam vīsitāvī.
7 Memor ad maiōrēs honōrēs ascendere volēbat.
8 in mediō oppidō labōrābant plūrimī fabrī, quī templum maximum exstruēbant.

4   You have also met another way of translating the superlative:

Rūfe, prūdentissimus es omnium amīcōrum quōs habeō.
Rufus, you are the shrewdest of all the friends that I have.

The following examples can be translated in the same way:

1 Bregāns erat stultissimus omnium servōrum quōs Salvius habēbat.
2 omnēs mīlitēs meī sunt fortēs; tū tamen fortissimus es.
3 postrēmō Athēnās vīsitāvimus, pulcherrimam omnium urbium.

Pronouns

1 ego and tū ('I', 'you', etc.)

	singular		*plural*	
nominative	ego	tū	nōs	vōs
accusative	mē	tē	nōs	vōs
dative	mihi	tibi	nōbīs	vōbīs

mēcum = 'with me'; tēcum = 'with you (singular)'
nōbīscum = 'with us'; vōbīscum = 'with you (plural)'

2 sē ('himself', 'herself', 'themselves', etc.)

	singular	*plural*
accusative	sē	sē
dative	sibi	sibi

'sēcum' ('with himself', etc.) is formed like 'mēcum', 'tēcum', etc. Notice some of the ways it can be translated:

tribūnus multōs comitēs sēcum habēbat.
The tribune had many companions with him.

Britannī uxōrēs sēcum dūcēbant.
The Britons were bringing their wives with them.

Agricola sēcum cōgitābat.
Agricola thought with himself.
    or, in much more natural English,
Agricola thought to himself.

3 hic ('this', 'these', etc.)

	singular			*plural*		
	masculine	*feminine*	*neuter*	*masculine*	*feminine*	*neuter*
nominative	hic	haec	hoc	hī	hae	haec
accusative	hunc	hanc	hoc	hōs	hās	haec
genitive		huius		hōrum	hārum	hōrum
dative		huic			hīs	

4 **ille** ('that', 'those', etc.; sometimes used with the meaning 'he', 'she', 'it', etc.)

	singular			*plural*		
	masculine	*feminine*	*neuter*	*masculine*	*feminine*	*neuter*
nominative	ille	illa	illud	illī	illae	illa
accusative	illum	illam	illud	illōs	illās	illa
genitive		illīus		illōrum	illārum	illōrum
dative		illī			illīs	

5 Notice the nominative case of the word for 'he', 'she', 'it', etc.:

	singular			*plural*		
	masculine	*feminine*	*neuter*	*masculine*	*feminine*	*neuter*
nominative	is	ea	id	eī	eae	ea
accusative	eum	eam	id	eōs	eās	ea
genitive		eius		eōrum	eārum	eōrum
dative		eī			eīs	

6 With the help of paragraphs 3–5 and (if necessary) the gender information in the table of nouns on pages 4 and 5, find the Latin for the words in italics in the following sentences:

1 I have never seen *that* girl before.
2 Guard *those* slaves!
3 *These* lions are dangerous.
4 I hate the noise of *this* city.
5 We shall give the prize to *this* boy.
6 We soon found *him*.
7 Where are the merchants? I want to see *them*.
8 Where is the temple? I want to see *it*.
9 Where is the city? I want to see *it*.
10 I hurried to *his* house.

7 From Stage 14 onwards you have met **ipse**. It can mean 'myself', 'yourself', 'himself', etc., depending on the word it is describing.

	singular			*plural*		
	masculine	*feminine*	*neuter*	*masculine*	*feminine*	*neuter*
nominative	ipse	ipsa	ipsum	ipsī	ipsae	ipsa
accusative	ipsum	ipsam	ipsum	ipsōs	ipsās	ipsa

sacerdōs ipse lacrimābat.
The priest himself was weeping.

fēmina mē ipsum accūsāvit.
The woman accused me myself.

Further examples:

1 ego ipse pugnam vīdī.
2 nōs ipsī in templō aderāmus.
3 subitō rēgem ipsum audīvimus.
4 dea ipsa mihi appāruit.

8 Notice the genitive and dative singular of the relative pronoun **quī**:

	singular			*plural*		
	masculine	*feminine*	*neuter*	*masculine*	*feminine*	*neuter*
nominative	quī	quae	quod	quī	quae	quae
accusative	quem	quam	quod	quōs	quās	quae
genitive		cuius		quōrum	quārum	quōrum
dative		cui			quibus	

senex cuius vīlla ardēbat magnōs clāmōrēs tollēbat.
The old man whose house was on fire was raising great shouts.

mercātor cui sellās mēnsāsque herī vēndidī hodiē revēnit.
The merchant to whom I sold chairs and tables yesterday came back today.

Further examples of the various forms of 'quī':

1 mīlitēs quōs Salvius ēmīsit tandem rediērunt.
2 iuvenis, cuius pater in Graeciā aberat, amīcōs ad cēnam sūmptuōsam invītāvit.
3 imperātor custōdēs quī dormīverant sevērissimē pūnīvit.
4 servus, cui sacerdōs signum dederat, duās victimās ad āram dūxit.
5 templum, quod in mediō oppidō stābat, saepe vīsitābam.
6 epistulam, quam nūntius tulerat, celeriter lēgī.

9 Sometimes the relative pronoun is used at the *beginning* of a sentence. Study the different ways of translating it:

Salviī amīcī īnsidiās Belimicō parāvērunt. quī, nihil suspicātus, ad aulam libenter vēnit.
Salvius' friends prepared a trap for Belimicus. He, having suspected nothing, came willingly to the palace.

tum pūmiliōnēs intrāvērunt. quōs cum vīdisset, puer rīsit.
Then the dwarfs entered. When he saw them, the boy laughed.

Cogidubnus 'grātiās vōbīs agō', inquit. quod cum dīxisset, cōnsēdit.
'Thank you', said Cogidubnus. When he had said this, he sat down.

In examples like these, the relative pronoun is said to be used as a *connecting relative*.

Further examples:

1 'cūr mihi nihil dās?' rogāvit Belimicus. quod cum audīvisset, Salvius īrātissimus erat.
2 tribūnus ancillīs pecūniam trādidit. quae, postquam dēnāriōs numerāvērunt, ad vīllam revēnērunt.
3 deinde rēx Memorī signum dedit. quī, togam praetextam gerēns, ad āram sollemniter prōcessit.
4 multī mīlitēs iam aulam complēbant. quōs cum vīdissent, sacerdōtēs surrēxērunt.

Verbs

1

first conjugation	*second conjugation*	*third conjugation*	*fourth conjugation*
PRESENT (INDICATIVE)			
I carry, you carry, etc.	*I teach, you teach, etc.*	*I drag, you drag, etc.*	*I hear, you hear, etc.*
portō	doceō	trahō	audiō
portās	docēs	trahis	audīs
portat	docet	trahit	audit
portāmus	docēmus	trahimus	audīmus
portātis	docētis	trahitis	audītis
portant	docent	trahunt	audiunt
IMPERFECT (INDICATIVE)			
I was carrying, you were carrying, etc.	*I was teaching, etc.*	*I was dragging, etc.*	*I was hearing, etc.*
portābam	docēbam	trahēbam	audiēbam
portābās	docēbās	trahēbās	audiēbās
portābat	*etc.*	*etc.*	*etc.*
portābāmus			
portābātis			
portābant			
PERFECT (INDICATIVE)			
I (have) carried, you (have) carried, etc.	*I (have) taught, etc.*	*I (have) dragged, etc.*	*I (have) heard, etc.*
portāvī	docuī	trāxī	audīvī
portāvistī	docuistī	trāxistī	audīvistī
portāvit	*etc.*	*etc.*	*etc.*
portāvimus			
portāvistis			
portāvērunt			
PLUPERFECT (INDICATIVE)			
I had carried, you had carried, etc.	*I had taught, etc.*	*I had dragged, etc.*	*I had heard, etc.*
portāveram	docueram	trāxeram	audīveram
portāverās	docuerās	trāxerās	audīverās
portāverat	*etc.*	*etc.*	*etc.*
portāverāmus			
portāverātis			
portāverant			

The word *indicative* (shown here in brackets) is sometimes included in the names of these tenses, to distinguish them from the present subjunctive, imperfect subjunctive, etc.

2 Translate each word. Then with the help of paragraph 1 change it into the present tense, keeping the same person and number (i.e. 1st person singular, etc.). Then translate again.

For example: 'portāverant' ('they had carried') would become
 'portant' ('they carry')
 and 'trāximus' ('we dragged') would become
 'trahimus' ('we drag').

1 docueram; trāxistī; portābāmus; audīvērunt.
2 ambulāverat; dormiēbam; laudāvimus; custōdīvistis.

3 You have also met the following forms of the verb:

1st conjugation	2nd conjugation	3rd conjugation	4th conjugation
INFINITIVE			
portāre	docēre	trahere	audīre
to carry	*to teach*	*to drag*	*to hear*
IMPERATIVE			
(s.) portā	docē	trahe	audī
(pl.) portāte	docēte	trahite	audīte
carry!	*teach!*	*drag!*	*hear!*
PRESENT PARTICIPLE			
portāns	docēns	trahēns	audiēns
carrying	*teaching*	*dragging*	*hearing*
PERFECT PASSIVE PARTICIPLE			
portātus	doctus	tractus	audītus
(having been)	*(having been)*	*(having been)*	*(having been)*
carried	*taught*	*dragged*	*heard*

4 You have also met some examples of the *perfect active* participle:

locūtus having spoken   secūtus having followed
    ingressus having entered

These examples all come from a particular group of verbs. The perfect active participle is the only part of these verbs that you have met so far.

5 For other forms of the present and perfect participles, and for examples of the ways in which they are used, see pp.176–77, 'Uses of the participle'.

Subjunctive forms

6 In Stages 24 and 25, you met two *subjunctive* tenses:

	first conjugation	*second conjugation*	*third conjugation*	*fourth conjugation*
IMPERFECT SUBJUNCTIVE				
1st person singular	portārem	docērem	traherem	audīrem
2nd person singular	portārēs	docērēs	traherēs	audīrēs
3rd person singular	portāret	*etc.*	*etc.*	*etc.*
1st person plural	portārēmus			
2nd person plural	portārētis			
3rd person plural	portārent			
PLUPERFECT SUBJUNCTIVE				
1st person singular	portāvissem	docuissem	trāxissem	audīvissem
2nd person singular	portāvissēs	docuissēs	trāxissēs	audīvissēs
3rd person singular	portāvisset	*etc.*	*etc.*	*etc.*
1st person plural	portāvissēmus			
2nd person plural	portāvissētis			
3rd person plural	portāvissent			

There are various ways of translating the subjunctive, depending on the way it is being used in a particular sentence (see pp.178–80, 'Uses of the subjunctive').

7 Complete each sentence with the right word and then translate.

1 intellegere nōn poteram cūr cīvēs portum . . . . . (peteret, peterent)

2 optiō in fossam dēsiluit ut hastās hostium . . . . . . (vītāret, vītārent)

3 senātor scīre voluit num pater meus . . . . . . (superfuisset, superfuissent)

4 cum senex tergum . . . . ., fūrēs per fenestram tacitē intrāvērunt. (vertisset, vertissent)

5 frātribus meīs tandem persuāsī ut ānulum aureum . . . . . . (redderet, redderent)

6 tanta erat nūbēs ut pāstōrēs sōlem vīdēre nōn . . . . . . (posset, possent)

Irregular verbs

1 You have now met the following forms of six irregular verbs:

esse *to be*	posse *to be able*	īre *to go*	velle *to want*	ferre *to bring*	capere *to take*

PRESENT (INDICATIVE)

I am, *you are, etc.*	*I am able,* *you are able,* *etc.*	*I go,* *you go,* *etc.*	*I want,* *you want,* *etc.*	*I bring,* *you bring,* *etc.*	*I take,* *you take,* *etc.*
sum	possum	eō	volō	ferō	capiō
es	potes	īs	vīs	fers	capis
est	potest	it	vult	fert	capit
sumus	possumus	īmus	volumus	ferimus	capimus
estis	potestis	ītis	vultis	fertis	capitis
sunt	possunt	eunt	volunt	ferunt	capiunt

IMPERFECT (INDICATIVE)

I was, *etc.*	*I was able,* *etc.*	*I was* *going, etc.*	*I was* *wanting, etc.*	*I was* *bringing, etc.*	*I was* *taking, etc.*
eram	poteram	ībam	volēbam	ferēbam	capiēbam
erās	poterās	ībās	volēbās	ferēbās	capiēbās
erat	*etc.*	*etc.*	*etc.*	*etc.*	*etc.*
erāmus					
erātis					
erant					

PERFECT (INDICATIVE)

I have *been, etc.*	*I have been* *able, etc.*	*I have* *gone, etc.*	*I (have)* *wanted, etc.*	*I (have)* *brought, etc.*	*I have* *taken, etc.*
fuī	potuī	iī	voluī	tulī	cēpī
fuistī	potuistī	iistī	voluistī	tulistī	cēpistī
fuit	*etc.*	*etc.*	*etc.*	*etc.*	*etc.*
fuimus					
fuistis					
fuērunt					

PLUPERFECT (INDICATIVE)

I had *been, etc.*	*I had been* *able, etc.*	*I had* *gone, etc.*	*I had* *wanted, etc.*	*I had* *brought, etc.*	*I had* *taken, etc.*
fueram	potueram	ieram	volueram	tuleram	cēperam
fuerās	potuerās	ierās	voluerās	tulerās	cēperās
fuerat	*etc.*	*etc.*	*etc.*	*etc.*	*etc.*
fuerāmus					
fuerātis					
fuerant					

IMPERFECT SUBJUNCTIVE

essem	possem	īrem	vellem	ferrem	caperem
essēs	possēs	īrēs	vellēs	ferrēs	caperēs
esset	*etc.*	*etc.*	*etc.*	*etc.*	*etc.*
essēmus					
essētis					
essent					

PLUPERFECT SUBJUNCTIVE

fuissem	potuissem	iissem	voluissem	tulissem	cēpissem
fuissēs	potuissēs	iissēs	voluissēs	tulissēs	cēpissēs
fuisset	*etc.*	*etc.*	*etc.*	*etc.*	*etc.*
fuissemus					
fuissētis					
fuissent					

2 Give the meaning of the following:

1 potes; vult; eō; it; fers; posse; fuī; potueram.
2 ībat; capiēbant; tulimus; cēpistis; fuerāmus; iistis; potuerant; poterant.

3 'capiō' is one of a group of verbs which belong to the third conjugation but behave in some ways like fourth conjugation verbs. Other verbs in this group are 'accipiō', 'faciō' and 'rapiō'.

Compare the infinitive of 'capiō' with the infinitive of 'trahō' (third conjugation) on p.171.

Compare the imperfect tense of 'capiō' with the imperfect tense of 'audiō' (fourth conjugation) on p.171.

Uses of the participle

1 In Stage 20 you met the *present participle*:

canis dominum **intrantem** vīdit.
The dog saw his master entering.

2 In Stage 21 you met the *perfect passive participle*:

servus, graviter **vulnerātus**, sub plaustrō iacēbat.
The slave, (having been) seriously wounded, was lȳing under the cart.

3 In Stage 22 you met the *perfect active participle*:

aegrōtī, deam **precātī**, remedium mīrābile spērābant.
The invalids, having prayed to the goddess, were hoping for a remarkable cure.

4 Translate the following examples. Pick out the participle in each sentence and say whether it is present, perfect passive or perfect active:

1 Latrō, prope iānuam tabernae stāns, pugnam spectābat.
2 Vilbia, ē culīnā ēgressa, sorōrem statim quaesīvit.
3 fūrēs, ad iūdicem ductī, veniam petīvērunt.
4 centuriō, amphoram vīnī optimī adeptus, ad amīcōs celeriter rediit.
5 subitō equōs appropinquantēs audīvimus.
6 puer callidus pecūniam, in terrā cēlātam, invēnit.

A participle is used to describe a noun. For example, in sentence 1 above, 'stāns' ('standing') describes 'Latrō'. Find the nouns described by the participles in sentences 2–6.

5 A participle agrees with the noun it describes in three ways: case, number and gender. For example:

nominative: **rēx**, in mediā turbā **sedēns**, dōna accipiēbat.
accusative: Quīntus **rēgem**, in mediā turbā **sedentem,** agnōvit.
singular: **lēgātus**, ad carcerem **regressus**, nēminem ibi invēnit.
plural: **custōdēs**, ad carcerem **regressī**, nēminem ibi invēnērunt.
masculine: **nūntius**, statim **profectus**, ad fundum contendit.
feminine: **uxor**, statim **profecta**, ad fundum contendit.

6   You have met the following forms of the *present participle*:

	singular		plural	
	masc. and fem.	*neuter*	*masc. and fem.*	*neuter*
nominative and vocative	trahēns	trahēns	trahentēs	trahentia
accusative	trahentem	trahēns	trahentēs	trahentia

Compare the endings of 'trahēns' with the endings of the adjective 'ingēns' on page 163.

7   You have met the following forms of the *perfect passive participle*:

	singular			plural		
	masculine	*feminine*	*neuter*	*masculine*	*feminine*	*neuter*
nominative and vocative	portātus (portāte)	portāta	portātum	portātī	portātae	portāta
accusative	portātum	portātam	portātum	portātōs	portātās	portāta

You have met the following forms of the *perfect active participle*:

	singular			plural		
	masculine	*feminine*	*neuter*	*masculine*	*feminine*	*neuter*
nominative and vocative	ingressus (ingresse)	ingressa	ingressum	ingressī	ingressae	ingressa
accusative	ingressum	ingressam	ingressum	ingressōs	ingressās	ingressa

Compare the endings of 'portātus' and 'ingressus' with the endings of the adjective 'bonus' on page 163.

8   With the help of paragraphs 6 and 7, find the Latin words for the participles in the following sentences:

1 I saw the soldiers dragging the slave to prison.
2 The girls, having been carried to safety, thanked their rescuers.
3 The king, having entered, greeted the chieftains.

Uses of the subjunctive

1 The forms of the imperfect and pluperfect subjunctive are given on p.172. The subjunctive can be used in several different ways, and its translation depends on the way it is being used in a particular sentence. In Unit IIIA you have met five uses of the subjunctive:

In Stage 24, you met the subjunctive used with 'cum' ('when'):

fabrī, cum pecūniam accēpissent, abiērunt.
When the workmen had received the money, they went away.

Further examples:

1 Agricola, cum legiōnem īnspexisset, mīlitēs centuriōnēsque laudāvit.
2 cum haruspex in templō cēnāret, rēx ipse appropinquābat.

2 In Stage 25, you met the subjunctive used in *indirect questions*:

cognōscere voluimus cūr multitūdō convēnisset.
We wanted to find out why the crowd had gathered.
(Compare this with the direct question:
'cūr multitūdō convēnit?' 'Why has the crowd gathered?')

Notice a new meaning of 'num' when used with an indirect question:

equitēs fēminās rogāvērunt num fugitīvōs vīdissent.
The horsemen asked the women whether they had seen the runaways.
(Compare this with the direct question:
'fugitīvōsne vīdistis?' 'Have you seen the runaways?')

Further examples:

1 incertus eram quam longum esset flūmen.
   (Compare: 'quam longum est flūmen?')
2 nēmō sciēbat num Memor lībertō venēnum praebuisset.
3 Rōmānī nesciēbant quot hostēs in castrīs manērent.
4 mē rogāvit num māter mea vīveret.

3 In Stage 26, you met the subjunctive used in *purpose clauses*:

senātor mē arcessīvit ut rem hospitibus nārrārem.
The senator summoned me in order that I might tell my story to
the guests.

Further examples:

1 amīcī ad urbem festīnāvērunt ut auxilium cīvibus ferrent.
2 epistulam scrīpsī ut lēgātum de perīculō monērem.

4 In Stage 27, you met the subjunctive used in *indirect commands*:

dominus nōbīs imperāvit ut sellās lectōsque emerēmus.
The master ordered us to buy chairs and couches.
(Compare this with the direct command:
'sellās lectōsque emite!' 'Buy chairs and couches!')

Further examples:

1 nūntius Britannīs persuāsit ut dōna ad aulam ferrent.
  (Compare: 'dōna ad aulam ferte!')
2 senex deam Sūlem ōrāvit ut morbum sānāret.

5 In Stage 27, you also met the subjunctive used in *result clauses*:

tanta erat stultitia iuvenum ut astrologō crēderent.
So great was the stupidity of the young men that they believed
the astrologer.

Further examples:

1 tam dīligenter carcerem custōdīvī ut lēgātus ipse mē laudāret.
2 mercātor tot vīllās habēbat ut eās numerāre nōn posset.

6 To understand why a subjunctive is being used in a particular sentence, it is necessary to look at the whole sentence, and not just the subjunctive on its own. For example, study these two sentences; one contains a *purpose* clause, and the other contains a *result* clause:

1 tam īrātus erat Agricola ut dormīre nōn posset.
  Agricola was so angry that he could not sleep.
2 Salvius mīlitēs ēmīsit ut Quīntum invenīrent.
  Salvius sent out the soldiers to find Quintus.

Sentence 1 clearly contains the result clause: Agricola's failure to sleep was the *result* of his anger. The word 'tam' ('so') is a further clue; it is often followed by a result clause later in the sentence. Other similar words are 'tantus' ('so great'), 'tot' ('so many') and 'adeō' ('so' or 'so much').

Sentence 2 clearly contains the purpose clause: finding Quintus was the *purpose* of sending out the soldiers.

7 Translate the following examples:

1 lībertus, cum venēnum bibisset, mortuus prōcubuit.
2 tot hostēs castra nostra oppugnābant ut dē vītā dēspērārēmus.
3 prīncipēs mē rogāvērunt cūr pontem trānsīre vellem.
4 Gutta sub mēnsā sē cēlāvit ut perīculum vītāret.
5 centuriōnēs mīlitibus imperāvērunt ut plaustra reficerent.
6 cum ancillae pōcula lavārent, quattuor equitēs ad tabernam advēnērunt.
7 adeō attonitus erat fīlius meus ut diū immōtus stāret.
8 iānuās cellārum aperuimus ut amīcōs nostrōs līberārēmus.
9 amīcus mē monuit ut latērem.
10 Modestus explicāre nōn poterat quō modō captīvī effūgissent.

In each sentence, find the reason why a subjunctive is being used.

Word order

1 In Unit I, you met the following word order:

dēspērābat senex.   The old man was in despair.

Further examples:
1 fūgit Modestus.   2 revēnērunt mercātōrēs.

2 From Stage 21 onwards, you have met the following word order:

dedit signum haruspex.   The soothsayer gave the signal.

Further examples:
1 rapuērunt pecūniam fūrēs.   2 īnspiciēbat mīlitēs Agricola.

3 From Stage 23 onwards, you have met the following word order:

ēmīsit Salvius equitēs.   Salvius sent out horsemen.

Further examples:
1 tenēbat Cephalus pōculum.   2 posuērunt cīvēs statuam.

4 Further examples of all three types of word order:

1 discessit nūntius.   4 poposcit captīvus lībertātem.
2 fēcērunt hostēs impetum.   5 vexābant mē puerī.
3 reficiēbat mūrum faber.   6 periērunt īnfantēs.

5 Study the word order in the following examples:

in hāc prōvinciā   ad nostrum patrem
in this province   to our father

From Stage 24 onwards, you have met a different word order:

mediīs in undīs   hanc ad tabernam
in the middle of the waves   to this shop

Further examples:

1 hāc in urbe   4 omnibus cum legiōnibus
2 multīs cum mīlitibus   5 tōtam per noctem
3 parvum ad oppidum   6 mediō in flūmine

Longer sentences

1 Study the following groups of sentences:

1a puerī timēbant.
The boys were afraid.

1b puerī timēbant quod prope iānuam iacēbat ingēns canis.
The boys were afraid because near the door was lying a huge dog.

1c puerī timēbant quod prope iānuam iacēbat ingēns canis, vehementer lātrāns.
The boys were afraid because near the door was lying a huge dog, barking loudly.

2a Strȳthiōnem cōnspexit.
He caught sight of Strythio.

2b ubi ā culīnā redībat, Strȳthiōnem cōnspexit.
When he was returning from the kitchen, he caught sight of Strythio.

2c ubi ā culīnā in quā cēnāverat redībat, Strȳthiōnem cōnspexit.
When he was returning from the kitchen in which he had been dining, he caught sight of Strythio.

3a Salvius incertus erat.
Salvius was uncertain.

3b Salvius incertus erat quō fūgisset Dumnorix.
Salvius was uncertain where Dumnorix had fled to.

3c Salvius incertus erat quō fūgisset Dumnorix, cūr abesset Quīntus.
Salvius was uncertain where Dumnorix had fled to, and why Quintus was missing.

2 Further examples:

4a centuriō immōtus manēbat.
4b centuriō immōtus manēbat, quamquam appropinquābant hostēs.
4c centuriō immōtus manēbat, quamquam appropinquābant hostēs, quī hastās vibrābant.

5a omnēs cīvēs plausērunt.
5b ubi puellae cantāre coepērunt, omnēs cīvēs plausērunt.
5c ubi puellae, quae prō pompā ambulābant, cantāre coepērunt, omnēs cīvēs plausērunt.

6a nūntius prīncipia petīvit.
6b nūntius quī epistulam ferēbat prīncipia petīvit.
6c nūntius quī epistulam ferēbat, simulac ad castra advēnit, prīncipia petīvit.

3 Further examples of the longer ('c') types of sentences:

7 tantae erant flammae ut vīllam magnam dēlērent, quam architectus clārus aedificāverat.
8 lībertus cubiculum intrāre nōlēbat quod Memor, quī multum vīnum biberat, graviter iam dormiēbat.
9 Salvius, Belimicō diffīsus, tribūnum arcessīvit ut vērum cognōsceret.
10 postquam ad forum vēnimus, ubi mercātōrēs negōtium agere solēbant, rem mīrābilem vīdimus.
11 pater, cum fīliōs pōcula haurientēs cōnspexisset, vehementer saeviēbat.
12 explōrātōrēs mox cognōvērunt ubi hostēs castra posuissent, quot mīlitēs in castrīs essent, quis mīlitibus praeesset.

PART TWO: Words and phrases

Notes

1 Nouns and adjectives are listed as in the Unit IIB Language Information section.

2 Verbs are usually listed in the following way:

the 1st person singular of the present tense, e.g. pōnō ('I place');
the infinitive, e.g. pōnere ('to place');
the 1st person singular of the perfect tense, e.g. posuī ('I placed');
the perfect passive participle, e.g. positus ('having been placed');
the meaning(s).

3 Study the following examples, listed in the way described in paragraph 2. Notice in particular the typical ways in which the different conjugations form their perfect tense and perfect passive participle.

first conjugation
amō, amāre, amāvī, amātus – love, like
laudō, laudāre, laudāvī, laudātus – praise

second conjugation
moneō, monēre, monuī, monitus – warn
praebeō, praebēre, praebuī, praebitus – provide

third conjugation
Verbs of the third conjugation form their perfect tense and perfect passive participle in several different ways. Here are some of them:

dūcō, dūcere, dūxī, ductus – lead
neglegō, neglegere, neglēxī, neglēctus – neglect
claudō, claudere, clausī, clausus – shut, close
mittō, mittere, mīsī, missus – send
frangō, frangere, frēgī, frāctus – break
relinquō, relinquere, relīquī, relictus – leave

fourth conjugation
custōdiō, custōdīre, custōdīvī, custōdītus – guard
impediō, impedīre, impedīvī, impedītus – hinder

4 Use paragraph 3 to find the meaning of:

amāvī, laudātus, monitus, praebēre, ductus, neglēxī, clausus, mīsī, frangere, frēgī, relinquō, relictus, custōdītus, impedīvī.

5 Use the list on pages 185–207 to find the meaning of:

adiuvāre, comprehēnsus, nocēre, pāreō, patefēcī, prōditus, suscēpī, ūnctus.

6 Some verbs have a perfect *active* participle, e.g. 'locūtus' ('having spoken'). You have not yet met any other forms of these verbs and so their perfect active participle is the only form listed in this pamphlet.

7 All words which are given in the 'Words and phrases checklists' for Stages 1–28 are marked with an asterisk.

a

*ā, ab – from; by
abdūcō, abdūcere, abdūxī, abductus
   – lead away
*abeō, abīre, abiī – go away
absēns, *gen.* absentis – absent
abstulī *see* auferō
*absum, abesse, āfuī – be out, be
   absent, be away
absurdus, absurda, absurdum –
   absurd
*ac – and
*accidō, accidere, accidī – happen
*accipiō, accipere, accēpī, acceptus –
   accept, take in, receive
accurrō, accurrere, accurrī – run up
*accūsō, accūsāre, accūsāvī, accūsātus
   – accuse
*ad – to, at
addō, addere, addidī, additus – add
addūcō, addūcere, addūxī, adductus
   – lead, lead on, encourage
*adeō, adīre, adiī – approach,
   go up to
*adeō – so much, so greatly
*adeptus, adepta, adeptum – having
   received, having obtained
adest *see* adsum
adhibeō, adhibēre, adhibuī,
   adhibitus – use, apply
   precēs adhibēre – offer prayers to
adhūc – up till now
*aditus, aditūs, m. – entrance
*adiuvō, adiuvāre, adiūvī – help

*administrō, administrāre,
   administrāvī, administrātus –
   look after, manage
adōrō, adōrāre, adōrāvī, adōrātus –
   worship
*adstō, adstāre, adstitī – stand by
*adsum, adesse, adfuī – be here, be
   present
*adveniō, advenīre, advēnī – arrive
*adventus, adventūs, m. – arrival
advesperāscit, advesperāscere,
   advesperāvit – get dark, become
   dark
*aedificium, aedificiī, n. – building
*aedificō, aedificāre, aedificāvī,
   aedificātus – build
*aeger, aegra, aegrum – sick, ill
aegrōtus, aegrōtī, m. – invalid
Aegyptius, Aegyptia, Aegyptium –
   Egyptian
afferō, afferre, attulī, adlātus – bring
afficiō, afficere, affēcī, affectus –
   affect
afflīgō, afflīgere, afflīxī, afflīctus –
   afflict, hurt
ager, agrī, m. – field
*agitō, agitāre, agitāvī, agitātus –
   chase, hunt
*agmen, agminis, n. – column
   (of men), procession
agna, agnae, f. – lamb
*agnōscō, agnōscere, agnōvī, agnitus –
   recognise

*agō, agere, ēgī, āctus – do, act
  age! – come on!
* fābulam agere – act a play
* grātiās agere – thank, give thanks
* negōtium agere – do business, work
  officium agere – do one's duty
  persōnam agere – play a part
  vītam agere – lead a life
*agricola, agricolae, m. – farmer
ālea, āleae, f. – dice
*aliquis, aliquid – someone, something
  aliquid novī – something new
*alius, alia, aliud – other, another, else
  aliī . . . aliī – some . . . others
*alter, altera, alterum – the other,
    another, a second, the second
altus, alta, altum – deep
amārus, amāra, amārum – bitter
ambō, ambae, ambō – both
*ambulō, ambulāre, ambulāvī – walk
amīcitia, amīcitiae, f. – friendship
*amīcus, amīcī, m. – friend
*āmittō, āmittere, āmīsī, āmissus –
  lose
*amō, amāre, amāvī, amātus – love,
  like
*amor, amōris, m. – love
amphora, amphorae, f. – wine-jar
amulētum, amulētī, n. – amulet,
  lucky charm
*ancilla, ancillae, f. – slave-girl, maid
angulus, angulī, m. – corner
angustus, angusta, angustum –
  narrow
*animus, animī, m. – spirit, soul, mind
  in animō volvere – wonder, turn
  over in the mind
*annus, annī, m. – year
ante – before, in front of
*anteā – before
*antīquus, antīqua, antīquum – old,
  ancient
*ānulus, ānulī, m. – ring
anxius, anxia, anxium – anxious
*aperiō, aperīre, aperuī, apertus –
  open

apertē – openly
apodytērium, apodytēriī, n. –
  changing-room
*appāreō, appārēre, appāruī – appear
*appropinquō, appropinquāre,
  appropinquāvī – approach,
  come near to
aptus, apta, aptum – suitable
*apud – among, at the house of
*aqua, aquae, f. – water
Aquae Sūlis, Aquārum Sūlis, f.pl
  – Bath
*āra, ārae, f. – altar
arānea, arāneae, f. – spider, spider's
  web
arca, arcae, f. – strong-box, chest
*accessō, arcessere, arcessīvī,
  arcessitus – summon, send for
architectus, architectī, m. – builder,
  architect
*ardeō, ardēre, arsī – burn, be on fire
ārea, āreae, f. – courtyard
*argenteus, argentea, argenteum –
  made of silver
arma, armōrum, n.pl. – arms,
  weapons
armārium, armāriī, n. – chest,
  cupboard
armātus, armāta, armātum – armed
*arrogantia, arrogantiae, f. – cheek,
  arrogance
*ars, artis, f. – art, skill
*ascendō, ascendere, ascendī – climb,
  rise
asinus, asinī, m. – ass, donkey
aspiciō, aspicere, aspexī – look
  towards
astrologus, astrologī, m. – astrologer
Athēnae, Athēnārum, f.pl. – Athens
*atque – and
*ātrium, ātriī, n. – hall
*attonitus, attonita, attonitum –
  astonished
*auctōritās, auctōritātis, f. – authority
auctus *see* augeō

audācia, audāciae, f. – boldness,
   audacity
audācter – boldly
*audāx, *gen.* audācis – bold, daring
*audeō, audēre – dare
   ausim – I should dare
*audiō, audīre, audīvī, audītus – hear
*auferō, auferre, abstulī, ablātus –
   take away, steal
augeō, augēre, auxī, auctus –
   increase
*aula, aulae, f. – palace

*aureus, aurea, aureum – golden,
   made of gold
aureus, aureī, m. – gold coin, gold
   piece
*auris, auris, f. – ear
*autem – but
*auxilium, auxiliī, n. – help
   auxiliō esse – be a help, be helpful
avāritia, avāritiae, f. – greed
*avārus, avārī, m. – miser
avē atque valē – hail and farewell
*avidē – eagerly
avidus, avida, avidum – eager

b

balneum, balneī, n. – bath
barba, barbae, f. – beard
barbarus, barbara, barbarum –
   barbarian
*barbarus, barbarī, m. – barbarian
*bellum, bellī, n. – war
*   bellum gerere – wage war,
   campaign
*bene – well
   optimē – very well
*beneficium, beneficiī, n. – act of
   kindness, favour
benignē – kindly
*benignus, benigna, benignum – kind
bēstia, bēstiae, f. – wild beast
*bibō, bibere, bibī – drink
blanditiae, blanditiārum, f.pl. –
   flatteries

blandus, blanda, blandum –
   flattering
*bonus, bona, bonum – good
   bona, bonōrum, n.pl. – goods
*   melior, melius – better
   melius est – it would be better
*   optimus, optima, optimum – very
   good, excellent, best
bracchium, bracchiī, n. – arm
brevī – in a short time
brevis, breve – short, brief
Britannī, Britannōrum, m.pl. –
   Britons
Britannia, Britanniae, f. – Britain
Britannicus, Britannica,
   Britannicum – British

c

C. = Gāius
cachinnō, cachinnāre, cachinnāvī –
   laugh, cackle
cadō, cadere, cecidī – fall
caecus, caeca, caecum – blind
*caedō, caedere, cecīdī, caesus – kill
*caelum, caelī, n. – sky
calceus, calceī, m. – shoe

Calēdonia, Calēdoniae, f. – Scotland
calliditās, calliditātis, f. – cleverness,
   shrewdness
*callidus, callida, callidum – clever,
   cunning, shrewd
*canis, canis, m. – dog
*cantō, cantāre, cantāvī – sing, chant
capillī, capillōrum, m.pl. – hair

*capiō, capere, cēpī, captus – take,
  catch, capture
  cōnsilium capere – make a plan,
  have an idea
*captīvus, captīvī, m. – prisoner,
  captive
*caput, capitis, n. – head
*carcer, carceris, m. – prison
  carnifex, carnificis, m. – executioner
*cārus, cāra, cārum – dear
  casa, casae, f. – small house
*castīgō, castīgāre, castīgāvī,
  castīgātus – scold
*castra, castrōrum, n.pl. – camp
  catēna, catēnae, f. – chain
  caudex, caudicis, m. – blockhead,
  idiot
  caupō, caupōnis, m. – innkeeper
  causa, causae, f. – reason, cause
*cautē – cautiously
  cecidī *see* cadō
*cēdō, cēdere, cessī – give in, give way
*celebrō, celebrāre, celebrāvī,
  celebrātus – celebrate
  celer, celeris, celere – quick, fast
  celerrimus, celerrima, celerrimum
  – very fast
*celeriter – quickly, fast
  celerrimē – very quickly, very fast
  quam celerrimē – as quickly as
  possible
  cella, cellae, f. – cell, sanctuary
*cēlō, cēlāre, cēlāvī, cēlātus – hide
*cēna, cēnae, f. – dinner
*cēnō, cēnāre, cēnāvī – dine, have
  dinner
*centum – a hundred
*centuriō, centuriōnis, m. – centurion
  cēpī *see* capiō
*cēra, cērae, f. – wax, wax tablet
*certāmen, certāminis, n. – struggle,
  fight
  certus, certa, certum – certain,
  infallible
  prō certō habēre – know for certain
  cessī *see* cēdō

*cēterī, cēterae, cētera – the others,
  the rest
*cibus, cibī, m. – food
*cinis, cineris, m. – ash
*circum – around
*circumspectō, circumspectāre,
  circumspectāvī – look round
  circumveniō, circumvenīre,
  circumvēnī, circumventus –
  surround
*cīvis, cīvis, m.f. – citizen
  clam – secretly, in private
*clāmō, clāmāre, clāmāvī – shout
*clāmor, clāmōris, m. – shout, uproar
*clārus, clāra, clārum – famous,
  distinguished
*claudō, claudere, clausī, clausus –
  shut, close, block
  clēmēns, *gen.* clēmentis – merciful
  Cn. = Gnaeus
*coepī – I began
*cōgitō, cōgitāre, cōgitāvī – think,
  consider
  sēcum cōgitāre – consider to
  himself
*cognōscō, cognōscere, cognōvī,
  cognitus – get to know, find out
*cōgō, cōgere, coēgī, coāctus – force,
  compel
*cohors, cohortis, f. – cohort
*colligō, colligere, collēgī, collēctus –
  gather, collect, assemble
*collocō, collocāre, collocāvī,
  collocātus – place, put
*colloquium, colloquiī, n. – talk, chat
  colō, colere, coluī, cultus – seek favour
  of, make friends with
  columna, columnae, f. – pillar
*comes, comitis, m.f. – comrade,
  companion
  cōmiter – politely, courteously
  commeātus, commeātūs, m. – leave
*commemorō, commemorāre,
  commemorāvī – talk about,
  mention, recall
  committō, committere, commīsī,
  commissus – commit, begin

*commodus, commoda, commodum –
   convenient
*commōtus, commōta, commōtum –
   moved, upset, affected, alarmed,
   excited, distressed, overcome
*comparō, comparāre, comparāvī,
   comparātus – obtain
*compleō, complēre, complēvī,
   complētus – fill
*comprehendō, comprehendere,
   comprehendī, comprehēnsus –
   arrest
conciliō, conciliāre, conciliāvī,
   conciliatus – win, gain
*cōnficiō, cōnficere, cōnfēcī, cōnfectus
   – finish
*cōnfīdō, cōnfīdere – trust
coniciō, conicere, coniēcī, coniectus –
   hurl, throw
*coniūrātiō, coniūrātiōnis, f. – plot,
   conspiracy
coniūrō, coniūrāre, coniūrāvī – plot,
   conspire
*cōnscendō, cōnscendere, cōnscendī –
   climb on, embark on, go on
   board, mount
*cōnsentiō, cōnsentīre, cōnsēnsī –
   agree
cōnsīdō, cōnsīdere, cōnsēdī – sit
   down
*cōnsilium, cōnsiliī, n. – plan, idea,
   advice
   cōnsilium capere – make a plan,
   have an idea
*cōnsistō, cōnsistere, cōnstitī – stand
   one's ground, stand firm, halt,
   stop
cōnspectus, cōnspectūs, m. – sight
*cōnspicātus, cōnspicāta, cōnspicātum
   – having caught sight of
*cōnspiciō, cōnspicere, cōnspexī,
   cōnspectus – catch sight of
*cōnstituō, cōnstituere, cōnstituī,
   cōnstitūtus – decide
cōnsulō, cōnsulere, cōnsuluī,
   cōnsultus – consult

*cōnsūmō, cōnsūmere, cōnsūmpsī,
   cōnsūmptus – eat
contemnō, contemnere, contempsī,
   contemptus – reject, despise
*contendō, contendere, contendī –
   hurry
contentiō, contentiōnis, f. – argument
*contentus, contenta, contentum –
   satisfied
contineō, continēre, continuī –
   contain
continuus, continua, continuum –
   continuous, on end
contiō, contiōnis, f. – speech
contrā – against
contrārius, contrāria, contrārium –
   opposite
contumēlia, contumēliae, f. – insult,
   abuse
convalēscō, convalēscere, convaluī –
   get better, recover
*conveniō, convenīre, convēnī – come
   together, gather, meet
conversus, conversa, conversum –
   having turned
*coquō, coquere, coxī, coctus – cook
*coquus, coquī, m. – cook
*corpus, corporis, n. – body
corrumpō, corrumpere, corrūpī,
   corruptus – corrupt
*cotīdiē – every day
*crēdō, crēdere, crēdidī – trust,
   believe, have faith in
cremō, cremāre, cremāvī, cremātus –
   cremate
creō, creāre, creāvī, creātus – make,
   create
crīmen, crīminis, n. – charge
*crūdēlis, crūdēle – cruel
cruentus, cruenta, cruentum –
   covered in blood
*cubiculum, cubiculī, n. – bedroom
cucurrī *see* currō
cui – to whom, to which (*dative of* quī)
cuius – whose, of which (*genitive of*
   quī)

culīna, culīnae, f. – kitchen
*cum – (1) when
*cum – (2) with
*cupiō, cupere, cupīvī – want
*cūr? – why?
*cūra, cūrae, f. – care

*cūrō, cūrāre, cūrāvī – look after,
  supervise
*currō, currere, cucurrī – run
*custōdiō, custōdīre, custōdīvī,
  custōdītus – guard
*custōs, custōdis, m. – guard

d

damnō, damnāre, damnāvī,
  damnātus – condemn
dare see dō
*dē – from, down from; about
*dea, deae, f. – goddess
*dēbeō, dēbēre, dēbuī, dēbitus – owe,
  ought, should, must
*decem – ten
*decet – it is proper
  mē decet – I ought
*dēcidō, dēcidere, dēcidī – fall down
decimus, decima, decimum – tenth
*dēcipiō, dēcipere, dēcēpī, dēceptus –
  deceive, trick
*decōrus, decōra, decōrum – right,
  proper
dedī see dō
*dēfendō, dēfendere, dēfendī,
  dēfēnsus – defend
dēfīxiō, dēfīxiōnis, f. – curse
*dēiciō, dēicere, dēiēcī, dēiectus –
  throw down, throw
*deinde – then
*dēlectō, dēlectāre, dēlectāvī,
  dēlectātus – delight, please
*dēleō, dēlēre, dēlēvī, dēlētus – destroy
dēliciae, dēliciārum, f.pl. – darling
dēligō, dēligāre, dēligāvī, dēligātus –
  bind, tie, tie up, moor
dēmittō, dēmittere, dēmīsī, dēmissus
  – let down, lower
*dēmōnstrō, dēmōnstrāre,
  dēmōnstrāvī, dēmōnstrātus –
  point out, show
dēmoveō, dēmovēre, dēmōvī,
  dēmōtus – dismiss

dēnārius, dēnāriī, m. – a denarius
  (coin)
*dēnique – at last, finally
*dēnsus, dēnsa, dēnsum – thick
dēnūntiō, dēnūntiāre, dēnūntiāvī,
  dēnūntiātus – denounce, reveal
*dēpōnō, dēpōnere, dēposuī,
  dēpositus – put down, take off
*dērīdeō, dērīdēre, dērīsī – mock,
  jeer at
*dēscendō, dēscendere, dēscendī –
  go down, come down
*dēserō, dēserere, dēseruī, dēsertus
  – desert
*dēsiliō, dēsilīre, dēsiluī – jump down
*dēsinō, dēsinere – end, cease
*dēspērō, dēspērāre, dēspērāvī –
  despair
dēstinō, dēstināre, dēstināvī,
  dēstinātus – intend
dēstringō, dēstringere, dēstrīnxī,
  dēstrictus – draw (a sword)
dētestātus, dētestāta, dētestātum –
  having cursed
*deus, deī, m. – god
*   dī immortālēs! – heavens above!
  Dēva, Dēvae, f. – Chester
dēvorō, dēvorāre, dēvorāvī,
  dēvorātus – devour, eat up
*dīcō, dīcere, dīxī, dictus – say
*dictō, dictāre, dictāvī – dictate
*diēs, diēī, m. – day
*   diēs nātālis, diēī nātālis, m. –
  birthday
*difficilis, difficile – difficult
  difficillimus, difficillima,
    difficillimum – very difficult

difficultās, difficultātis, f. –
   difficulty
diffīsus, diffīsa, diffīsum – having
   distrusted
*dignitās, dignitātis, f. – importance,
   honour, prestige
dignus, digna, dignum – worthy,
   appropriate
dīlaniō, dīlaniāre, dīlaniāvī,
   dīlaniātus – tear to pieces
*dīligenter – carefully
*dīligentia, dīligentiae, f. – industry,
   hard work
*dīligō, dīligere, dīlēxī, dīlēctus – be
   fond of
*dīmittō, dīmittere, dīmīsī, dīmissus
   – send away, dismiss
dīrigō, dīrigere, dīrēxī, dīrēctus –
   steer
dīripiō, dīripere, dīripuī, dīreptus –
   pull apart, ransack
*dīrus, dīra, dīrum – dreadful
*discēdō, discēdere, discessī – depart,
   leave
disciplīna, disciplīnae, f. – discipline,
   orderliness
discordia, discordiae, f. – strife

*dissentiō, dissentīre, dissēnsī –
   disagree, argue
*diū – for a long time
   diūtius – any longer
dīxī *see* dīcō
*dō, dare, dedī, datus – give
   poenās dare – pay the penalty, be
   punished
*doceō, docēre, docuī, doctus – teach
*doctus, docta, doctum – learned,
   educated, skilful, clever
*doleō, dolēre, doluī – hurt, be in pain
   graviter dolēre – be extremely
   painful
dolus, dolī, m. – trickery
*domina, dominae, f. – mistress
*dominus, dominī, m. – master
*domus, domūs, f. – home
   domum redīre – return home
*dōnum, dōnī, n. – present, gift
*dormiō, dormīre, dormīvī – sleep
*ducentī, ducentae, ducenta – two
   hundred
*dūcō, dūcere, dūxī, ductus – lead
*dulcis, dulce – sweet
*duo, duae, duo – two
*dūrus, dūra, dūrum – harsh, hard

e

*ē, ex – from, out of
   ea – those things
   eādem – the same
   eam – her
   eās – them
   ēbrius, ēbria, ēbrium – drunk
*ecce! – see! look!
efferō, efferre, extulī, ēlātus – bring
   out, carry out
*efficiō, efficere, effēcī, effectus – carry
   out, accomplish
*effigiēs, effigiēī, f. – image, statue
*effugiō, effugere, effūgī – escape
effundō, effundere, effūdī, effūsus –
   pour out

*ego, meī – I, me
   mēcum – with me
*ēgressus, ēgressa, ēgressum – having
   gone out
*ēheu! – alas !
   eī – to him, to her, to it
ēiciō, ēicere, ēiēcī, ēiectus – throw out
   eīs – to them
   eius – his, of him
ēlāpsus, ēlāpsa, ēlāpsum – having
   escaped
*ēligō, ēligere, ēlēgī, ēlēctus – choose
*ēmittō, ēmittere, ēmīsī, ēmissus –
   throw, send out
*emō, emere, ēmī, ēmptus – buy

ēn! – look!
    ēn iūstitia! – so this is justice!
*enim – for
*eō, īre, iī – go
  eō – from him
  eōrum – their, of them
  eōs – them
*epistula, epistulae, f. – letter
*eques, equitis, m. – horseman
*equitō, equitāre, equitāvī – ride
*equus, equī, m. – horse
  eram *see* sum
  ēripiō, ēripere, ēripuī, ēreptus –
    snatch, tear
*errō, errāre, errāvī – make a mistake
  longē errāre – make a big mistake
  ērumpō, ērumpere, ērūpī, ēruptus –
    break away, break out
  est *see* sum
  ēsuriō, ēsurīre – be hungry
*et – and
  et . . . et – both . . . and
*etiam – even, also
  nōn sōlum . . . sed etiam – not only
    . . . but also
*euge! – hurray!
*eum – him
  ex, ē – from, out of
*exanimātus, exanimāta, exanimātum
  – unconscious
  excipiō, excipere, excēpī, exceptus –
    receive
*excitō, excitāre, excitāvī, excitātus –
  arouse, wake up, awaken

*exclāmō, exclāmāre, exclāmāvī –
  exclaim, shout
  excruciō, excruciāre, excruciāvī,
    excruciātus – torture, torment
*exeō, exīre, exiī – go out
*exerceō, exercēre, exercuī, exercitus –
  exercise
  exilium, exiliī, n. – exile
*exitium, exitiī, n. – ruin, destruction
  expellō, expellere, expulī, expulsus –
    throw out, drive out
*explicō, explicāre, explicāvī,
  explicātus – explain
  explōrātor, explōrātōris, m. – scout,
    spy
  exquīsītus, exquīsīta, exquīsītum –
    special
*exspectō, exspectāre, exspectāvī,
  exspectātus – wait for
  exstinguō, exstinguere, exstīnxī,
    exstīnctus – extinguish, destroy
  exstruō, exstruere, exstrūxī,
    exstrūctus – build
  exsultō, exsultāre, exsultāvī – exult,
    be triumphant
  extorqueō, extorquēre, extorsī,
    extortus – extort
*extrā – outside
*extrahō, extrahere, extrāxī, extractus
  – drag out, pull out, take out
  extulī *see* efferō
  exuō, exuere, exuī, exūtus – take off

f

*faber, fabrī, m. – craftsman
*fābula, fābulae, f. – play, story
*   fābulam agere – act a play
  facēs *see* fax
*facile – easily
*facilis, facile – easy
*facinus, facinoris, n. – crime

*faciō, facere, fēcī, factus – make, do
  floccī nōn faciō – I don't care a
    hang for
  impetum facere – charge, make an
    attack
  sēditiōnem facere – revolt
  fallō, fallere, fefellī, falsus – deceive

falsum, falsī, n. – lie
*falsus, falsa, falsum – false, untrue,
  dishonest
*familiāris, familiāris, m. – relation,
  relative
*faveō, favēre, fāvī – favour, support
  favor, favōris, m. – favour
*fax, facis, f. – torch
  fēcī *see* faciō
  fefellī *see* fallō
  fēlēs, fēlis, f. – cat
*fēmina, fēminae, f. – woman
  fenestra, fenestrae, f. – window
*ferō, ferre, tulī, lātus – bring, carry
  graviter ferre – take badly
*ferōciter – fiercely
*ferōx, *gen.* ferōcis – fierce, ferocious
*fessus, fessa, fessum – tired
*festīnō, festīnāre, festīnāvī – hurry
  fibula, fibulae, f. – brooch
*fidēlis, fidēle – faithful, loyal
*fidēs, fideī, f. – loyalty,
  trustworthiness
  fidus, fīda, fīdum – loyal, trustworthy
*fīlia, fīliae, f. – daughter
*fīlius, fīliī, m. – son
  fingō, fingere, finxī, fictus – invent,
  pretend
  fiō – I become
*flamma, flammae, f. – flame
  floccī nōn faciō – I don't care a hang
  for
*flōs, flōris, m. – flower

*flūmen, flūminis, n. – river
*fluō, fluere, flūxī – flow
*fōns, fontis, m. – fountain, spring
*fortasse – perhaps
*forte – by chance
*fortis, forte – brave
*fortiter – bravely
*fortūna, fortūnae, f. – fortune, luck
  fortūnātus, fortūnāta, fortūnātum –
  lucky
*forum, forī, n. – forum, market-place
*fossa, fossae, f. – ditch
*frangō, frangere, frēgī, frāctus – break
*frāter, frātris, m. – brother
  fraus, fraudis, f. – trick
*frūmentum, frūmentī, n. – grain
*frūstrā – in vain
  fuga, fugae, f. – escape
*fugiō, fugere, fūgī – run away, flee
  (from)
  fugitivus, fugitīvī, m. – fugitive,
  runaway
  fuī *see* sum
*fulgeō, fulgēre, fulsī – shine, glitter
*fundō, fundere, fūdī, fūsus – pour
*fundus, fundī, m. – farm
  fūnus, fūneris, n. – funeral
*fūr, fūris, m. – thief
  furcifer, furciferī, m. – scoundrel
*furēns, *gen.* furentis – furious, in a
  rage
  fūrtum, fūrtī, n. – theft, robbery
  fūstis, fūstis, m. – club, stick

g

garriō, garrīre, garrīvī – chatter,
  gossip
  garum, garī, n. – sauce
*gaudeō, gaudēre – be pleased, rejoice
*geminī, geminōrum, m.pl. – twins
*gemitus, gemitūs, m. – groan
*gemma, gemmae, f. – jewel, gem
*gēns, gentis, f. – family, tribe
  ubi gentium? – where in the world?
  genū, genūs, n. – knee

*gerō, gerere, gessī, gestus – wear
*   bellum gerere – wage war,
  campaign
  gladiātor, gladiātōris, m. – gladiator
*gladius, gladiī, m. – sword
  Graecia, Graeciae, f. – Greece
  Graecus, Graeca, Graecum – Greek
  grānum, grānī, n. – grain
  grātiae, grātiārum, f.pl. – thanks
*   grātiās agere – thank, give thanks

grātīs – free
*gravis, grave – heavy, serious
*graviter – heavily, soundly, seriously
    graviter dolēre – be extremely
    painful
    graviter ferre – take badly

gubernātor, gubernātōris, m. –
    helmsman
*gustō, gustāre, gustāvī – taste
guttur, gutturis, n. – throat

h

*habeō, habēre, habuī, habitus – have
    in memoriā habēre – keep in mind,
    remember
    minōris pretiī habēre – care less
    about
    prō certō habēre – know for
    certain
    prō hostibus habēre – reckon as
    enemies
    sermōnem habēre – have a
    conversation, talk
*habitō, habitāre, habitāvī – live
hāc, hae, haec see hic
*haereō, haerēre, haesī – stick, cling
*haesitō, haesitāre, haesitāvī – hesitate
hanc see hic
*haruspex, haruspicis, m. – soothsayer
hās see hic
*hasta, hastae, f. – spear
haud – not
haudquāquam – not at all
*hauriō, haurīre, hausī, haustus –
    drain, drink up
*hercle! – by Hercules!
*hērēs, hērēdis, m.f. – heir
herī – yesterday
heus! – hey!
*hic, haec, hoc – this

hīc – here
*hiems, hiemis, f. – winter
hilarē – in high spirits, merrily
hinc – from here
Hispānia, Hispāniae, f. – Spain
hoc, hōc see hic
*hodiē – today
*homō, hominis, m. – man
homunculus, homunculī, m. – little
    man
*honor, honōris, m. – honour, official
    position
*honōrō, honōrāre, honōrāvī – honour
*hōra, hōrae, f. – hour
*horreum, horreī, n. – barn, granary
hortātus, hortāta, hortātum – having
    encouraged
*hortus, hortī, m. – garden
hōrum see hic
*hospes, hospitis, m. – guest, host
*hostis, hostis, m.f. – enemy
*hūc – here, to this place
huic – to this (*dative of* hic)
huius – of this (*genitive of* hic)
humus, humī, f. – ground
*   humī – on the ground
hunc see hic

i

*iaceō, iacēre, iacuī – lie
*iaciō, iacere, iēcī, iactus – throw
*iactō, iactāre, iactāvī, iactātus –
    throw
*iam – now
*iānua, iānuae, f. – door
ībam *see* eō
*ibi – there
id – it
iecur, iecoris, n. – liver
*igitur – therefore, and so
*ignārus, ignāra, ignārum – not
    knowing, unaware
*ignāvus, ignāva, ignāvum – lazy,
    cowardly
ignōtus, ignōta, ignōtum – unknown
iī *see* eō
*ille, illa, illud – that, he, she
*illūc – there, to that place
*immemor, *gen.* immemoris – forgetful
immineō, imminēre, imminuī – hang
    over
*immortālis, immortāle – immortal
*   dī immortālēs ! – heavens above!
*immōtus, immōta, immōtum – still,
    motionless
impatiēns, *gen.* impatientis –
    impatient
*impediō, impedīre, impedīvī,
    impedītus – delay, hinder
impellō, impellere, impulī, impulsus
    – push, force
*imperātor, imperātōris, m. – emperor
*imperium, imperiī, n. – empire
*imperō, imperāre, imperāvī – order,
    command
*impetus, impetūs, m. – attack
    impetum facere – charge, make an
    attack
impōnō, impōnere, imposuī,
    impositus – impose
importō, importāre, importāvī,
    importātus – import
imprecātiō, imprecātiōnis, f. – curse

impulī *see* impellō
*in – in, on; into, onto
inānis, ināne – empty, meaningless
*incendō, incendere, incendī, incēnsus
    – burn, set fire to
incēnsus, incēnsa, incēnsum –
    inflamed, angered
incertus, incerta, incertum –
    uncertain
*incidō, incidere, incidī – fall
*incipiō, incipere, incēpī, inceptus –
    begin
*incitō, incitāre, incitāvī, incitātus –
    urge on, encourage
inclūsus, inclūsa, inclūsum – shut up,
    imprisoned, trapped
incurrō, incurrere, incurrī – run onto,
    collide with, bump into
indicium, indiciī, n. – sign, evidence
*induō, induere, induī, indūtus –
    put on
inest *see* īnsum
*īnfāns, īnfantis, m. – child, baby
*īnfēlīx, *gen.* īnfēlīcis – unlucky
*īnferō, īnferre, intulī, inlātus – bring
    in, bring on, bring against
*īnfestus, īnfesta, īnfestum – hostile,
    dangerous
*ingenium, ingeniī, n. – character
*ingēns, *gen.* ingentis – huge
ingravēscō, ingravēscere – grow
    worse
*ingressus, ingressa, ingressum –
    having entered
*iniciō, inicere, iniēcī, iniectus –
    throw in
inimīcitia, inimīcitiae, f. – feud,
    quarrel
*inimīcus, inimīcī, m. – enemy
iniūria, iniūriae, f. – injustice, injury
innīxus, innīxa, innīxum – having
    leant
innocēns, *gen.* innocentis – innocent

*inquit – says, said
  inquam – I said
īnsānia, īnsāniae, f. – madness,
  insanity
īnsāniō, īnsānīre, īnsānīvī – be mad,
  be insane
*īnsānus, īnsāna, īnsānum – mad,
  crazy, insane
*īnsidiae, īnsidiārum, f.pl. – trap,
  ambush
īnsolēns, *gen.* īnsolentis – rude,
  insolent
īnsolenter – rudely, insolently
*īnspiciō, īnspicere, īnspexī, īnspectus
  – look at, inspect, examine
*īnstruō, īnstruere, īnstrūxī, īnstrūctus
  – draw up
*īnsula, īnsulae, f. – island
īnsum, inesse, īnfuī – be inside
*intellegō, intellegere, intellēxī,
  intellēctus – understand
*intentē – intently
*inter – among
  inter sē – among themselves, with
    each other
*intereā – meanwhile
*interficiō, interficere, interfēcī,
  interfectus – kill
interrogō, interrogāre, interrogāvī,
  interrogātus – question
*intrō, intrāre, intrāvī – enter

1

L. = Lūcius
labefaciō, labefacere, labefēcī,
  labefactus – weaken
labor, labōris, m. – work
*labōrō, labōrāre, labōrāvī – work
labrum, labrī, n. – lip
lacertus, lacertī, m. – muscle
*lacrima, lacrimae, f. – tear
*lacrimō, lacrimāre, lacrimāvī – weep,
  cry
*laedō, laedere, laesī, laesus – harm
laetē – happily

intulī *see* īnferō
intus – inside
inultus, inulta, inultum – unavenged
*inveniō, invenīre, invēnī, inventus –
  find
*invītō, invītāre, invītāvī, invītātus –
  invite
*invītus, invīta, invītum – unwilling,
  reluctant
iō! – hurray!
*iocus, iocī, m. – joke
*ipse, ipsa, ipsum – himself, herself,
  itself
*īra, īrae, f. – anger
*īrātus, īrāta, īrātum – angry
īre *see* eō
*irrumpō, irrumpere, irrūpī, irruptus
  – burst in, burst into
*iste, ista, istud – that
*ita – in this way
*ita vērō – yes
Ītalia, Ītaliae, f. – Italy
*itaque – and so
*iter, itineris, n. – journey, progress
*iterum – again
*iubeō, iubēre, iussī, iussus – order
*iūdex, iūdicis, m. – judge
iugulum, iugulī, n. – throat
*iussum, iussī, n. – order, instruction
iūstitia, iūstitiae, f. – justice
*iuvenis, iuvenis, m. – young man

*laetus, laeta, laetum – happy
lāpsus, lāpsa, lāpsum – having fallen
*lateō, latēre, latuī – lie hidden
*latrō, latrōnis, m. – robber
*lātus, lāta, lātum – wide
*laudō, laudāre, laudāvī, laudātus –
  praise
*lavō, lavāre, lāvī, lautus – wash
*lectus, lectī, m. – couch, bed
*lēgātus, lēgātī, m. – commander
lēgibus *see* lēx
*legiō, legiōnis, f. – legion

lēgō, lēgāre, lēgāvī, lēgātus –
  bequeath
*legō, legere, lēgī, lēctus – read
*lentē – slowly
*leō, leōnis, m. – lion
leviter – lightly, slightly
lēx, lēgis, f. – law
libellus, libellī, m. – little book
*libenter – gladly
*liber, librī, m. – book
*līberālis, līberāle – generous
līberī, līberōrum, m.pl. – children
*līberō, līberāre, līberāvī,
  līberātus – free, set free
libertās, libertātis, f. – freedom
*lībertus, lībertī, m. – freedman,
  ex-slave

librōs *see* liber
*lingua, linguae, f. – tongue
*lītus, lītoris, n. – sea-shore, shore
līvidus, līvida, līvidum –
  lead-coloured
*locus, locī, m. – place
*locūtus, locūta, locūtum – having
  spoken
longē – far
  longē errāre – make a big mistake
*longus, longa, longum – long
loquāx, *gen.* loquācis – talkative
lucerna, lucernae, f. – lamp
lūdō, lūdere, lūsī – play
*lūna, lūnae, f. – moon

m

madidus, madida, madidum – soaked
magicus, magica, magicum – magic
*magnopere – greatly
  maximē – very greatly, very much,
    most of all
*magnus, magna, magnum – big,
    large, great
  maior, *gen.* maiōris – bigger,
    larger, greater
  maximus, maxima, maximum –
    very big, very large, very great
maiestās, maiestātis, f. – treason
maior, *gen.* maiōris – bigger, larger,
  greater
mālim – I should prefer
*malus, mala, malum – evil, bad
  peior, *gen.* peiōris – worse
  pessimus, pessima, pessimum –
    worst, very bad
*mandātum, mandātī, n. –
  instruction, order
*mandō, mandāre, mandāvī,
  mandātus – order, entrust, hand
  over
*māne – in the morning
*maneō, manēre, mānsī – remain, stay

*manus, manūs, f. – (1) hand
*manus, manūs, f. – (2) band
*mare, maris, n. – sea
*marītus, marītī, m. – husband
  Mārs, Mārtis, m. – Mars (god of war)
*māter, mātris, f. – mother
mātrimōnium, mātrimōniī, n. –
  marriage
*maximē – very greatly, very much,
    most of all
*maximus, maxima, maximum – very
    big, very large, very great
mē *see* ego
*medicus, medicī, m. – doctor
*medius, media, medium – middle
*melior – better
  melius est – it would be better
memoria, memoriae, f. – memory
  in memoriā habēre – keep in mind,
    remember
*mendāx, mendācis, m. – liar
mendāx, *gen.* mendācis – lying,
  deceitful
*mēnsa, mēnsae, f. – table
mēnsis, mēnsis, m. – month
*mercātor, mercātōris, m. – merchant

meritus, merita, meritum –
　well-deserved
*metus, metūs, m. – fear
*meus, mea, meum – my, mine
　mī Quīnte – my dear Quintus
mihi *see* ego
*mīles, mīlitis, m. – soldier
mīlitō, mīlitāre, mīlitāvī – be a
　soldier
*mīlle – a thousand
*　mīlia – thousands
*minimē – no, least, very little
*minimus, minima, minimum – very
　little, least
minor, *gen.* minōris – less, smaller
*mīrābilis, mīrābile – marvellous,
　strange, wonderful
misceō, miscēre, miscuī, mixtus – mix
*miser, misera, miserum – miserable,
　wretched, sad
　o mē miserum! – O wretched me!
*mittō, mittere, mīsī, missus – send
*modus, modī, m. – manner, way, kind
　quō modō ? – how? in what way?
　rēs huius modī – a thing of this kind
*molestus, molesta, molestum –
　troublesome

molliō, mollīre, mollīvī, mollītus –
　soothe
mollis, molle – soft, gentle
mōmentum, mōmentī, n. –
　importance
*moneō, monēre, monuī, monitus –
　warn, advise
*mōns, montis, m. – mountain
mora, morae, f. – delay
*morbus, morbī, m. – illness
　(eī) moriendum est – (he) must die
*mors, mortis, f. – death
*mortuus, mortua, mortuum – dead
mōs, mōris, m. – custom
*mox – soon
*multitūdō, multitūdinis, f. – crowd
*multō – much
*multus, multa, multum – much
*　multī – many
*　plūs, *gen.* plūris – more
*　plūrimī, plūrimae, plūrima – very
　many
*　plūrimus, plūrima, plūrimum –
　most
*mūrus, mūrī, m. – wall
mūs, mūris, m.f. – mouse

n

*nam – for
*nārrō, nārrāre, nārrāvī, nārrātus –
　tell, relate
nāsus, nāsī, m. – nose
*(diēs) nātālis, (diēī) nātālis, m. –
　birthday
*nauta, nautae, m. – sailor
*nāvigō, nāvigāre, nāvigāvī – sail
*nāvis, nāvis, f. – ship
*necesse – necessary
*necō, necāre, necāvī, necātus – kill
*neglegēns, *gen.* neglegentis – careless
neglegō, neglegere, neglēxī,
　neglēctus – neglect
*negōtium, negōtiī, n. – business
*　negōtium agere – do business, work

*nēmō – no one, nobody
neque – and not
*　neque . . . neque – neither . . . nor
*nescio, nescīre, nescīvī – not know
niger, nigra, nigrum – black
*nihil – nothing
　nihil perīculī – no danger
nimis – too
*nimium – too much
*nōbilis, nōbile – noble, of noble birth
nōbīs *see* nōs
nocēns, *gen.* nocentis – guilty
*noceō, nocēre, nocuī – hurt
noctū – by night
*nōlō, nōlle, nōluī – not want
　nōlī, nōlīte – do not, don't

*nōmen, nōminis, n. – name
*nōn – not
*nōnāgintā – ninety
*nōnne? – surely?
*nōnnūllī, nōnnūllae, nōnnūlla –
    some, several
nōnus, nōna, nōnum – ninth
*nōs – we, us
*noster, nostra, nostrum – our
*nōtus, nōta, nōtum – known, well-
    known, famous
*novem – nine
*nōvī – I know
*novus, nova, novum – new

*nox, noctis, f. – night
    noctū – by night
*nūbēs, nūbis, f. – cloud
*nūllus, nūlla, nūllum – not any, no
*num? –(1) surely . . . not?
*num – (2) whether
*numerō, numerāre, numerāvī,
    numerātus – count
*numerus, numerī, m. – number
*numquam – never
*nunc – now
*nūntiō, nūntiāre, nūntiāvī,
    nūntiātus – announce
*nūntius, nūntiī, m. – messenger
*nūper – recently
*nusquam – nowhere

O

obdormiō, obdormīre, obdormīvī –
    go to sleep
obēsus, obēsa, obēsum – fat
obscūrus, obscūra, obscūrum –
    dark, gloomy
obstinātus, obstināta, obstinātum –
    stubborn
*obstō, obstāre, obstitī – obstruct,
    block the way
obtulī *see* offerō
obviam eō, obviam īre, obviam iī –
    meet, go to meet
*occīdō, occīdere, occīdī, occīsus – kill
*occupātus, occupāta, occupātum –
    busy
*occupō, occupāre, occupāvī,
    occupātus – seize, take over
*occurrō, occurrere, occurrī – meet
*octō – eight
*octōgintā – eighty
*oculus, oculī, m. – eye
    ōdī – I hate
*offerō, offerre, obtulī, oblātus – offer
officium, officiī, n. – duty
    officium agere – do one's duty

*ōlim – once, some time ago
ōmen, ōminis, n. – omen (sign from
    the gods)
omittō, omittere, omīsī, omissus –
    drop, leave out, omit
omnīnō – completely
*omnis, omne – all
    omnia – all, everything
*opēs, opum, f.pl. – money, wealth
*oportet – it is right
    mē oportet – I must
*oppidum, oppidī, n. – town
opprimō, opprimere, oppressī,
    oppressus – crush
*oppugnō, oppugnāre, oppugnāvī,
    oppugnātus – attack
*optimē – very well
*optimus, optima, optimum – very
    good, excellent, best
optiō, optiōnis, m. – optio (military
    officer ranking below centurion)
*ōrdō, ōrdinis, m. – row, line
ōrnāmentum, ōrnāmentī, n. –
    ornament, decoration
ōrnātus, ōrnāta, ōrnātum –
    decorated, elaborately furnished

*ōrnō, ōrnāre, ōrnāvī, ōrnātus –
    decorate
ōrō, ōrāre, ōrāvī – beg
*ōs, ōris, n. – face

*ōsculum, ōsculī, n. – kiss
*ostendō, ostendere, ostendī,
    ostentus – show

p

*paene – nearly, almost
pallēscō, pallēscere, palluī – grow
    pale
*pallidus, pallida, pallidum – pale
pallium, palliī, n. – cloak
pālus, pālī, m. – stake, post
*parātus, parāta, parātum – ready,
    prepared
*parcō, parcere, pepercī – spare
*parēns, parentis, m.f. – parent
*pāreō, pārēre, pāruī – obey
*parō, parāre, parāvī, parātus –
    prepare
*pars, partis, f. – part
*parvus, parva, parvum – small
    minor, *gen.* minōris – less,
    smaller
*   minimus, minima, minimum –
    very little, least
*passus, passa, passum – having
    suffered
pāstor, pāstōris, m. – shepherd
*patefaciō, patefacere, patefēcī,
    patefactus – reveal
*pater, patris, m. – father
patera, paterae, f. – bowl
patientia, patientiae, f. – patience
*paucī, paucae, pauca – few, a few
*paulīsper – for a short time
paulō – a little
*pāx, pācis, f. – peace
*pecūnia, pecūniae, f. – money
peior, *gen.* peiōris – worse
*per – through
perdomitus, perdomita, perdomitum
    – conquered
*pereō, perīre, periī – die, perish
*perfidia, perfidiae, f. – treachery

*perfidus, perfida, perfidum –
    treacherous, untrustworthy
perfuga, perfugae, m. – deserter
*perīculōsus, perīculōsa, perīculōsum
    – dangerous
*perīculum, perīculī, n. – danger
periī *see* pereō
perītē – skilfully
*perītus, perīta, perītum – skilful
permōtus, permōta, permōtum –
    alarmed, disturbed
perrumpō, perrumpere, perrūpī,
    perruptus – burst through,
    burst in
persecūtus, persecūta, persecūtum –
    having pursued
persōna, persōnae, f. – character
    persōnam agere – play a part
*persuādeō, persuādēre, persuāsī –
    persuade
*perterritus, perterrita, perterritum –
    terrified
perturbō, perturbāre, perturbāvī,
    perturbātus – disturb, alarm
*perveniō, pervenīre, pervēnī –
    reach, arrive at
*pēs, pedis, m. – foot, paw
pessimē – very badly
*pessimus, pessima, pessimum –
    worst, very bad
*pestis, pestis, f. – pest, scoundrel
*petō, petere, petīvī, petītus – make
    for, attack; seek, beg for, ask for
*placet, placēre, placuit – please, suit
*plaudō, plaudere, plausī, plausus –
    applaud, clap
*plaustrum, plaustrī, n. – wagon, cart
*plēnus, plēna, plēnum – full
pluit, pluere, pluit – rain

*plūrimus, plūrima, plūrimum – most
* plūrimī, plūrimae, plūrima – very
many
*plūs, *gen.* plūris – more
plūs vīnī – more wine
*pōculum, pōculī, n. – wine-cup
*poena, poenae, f. – punishment
* poenās dare – pay the penalty, be
punished
*poēta, poētae, m. – poet
poliō, polīre, polīvī, polītus – polish
*pompa, pompae, f. – procession
Pompēiānus, Pompēiāna,
Pompēiānum – Pompeian
*pōnō, pōnere, posuī, positus – put,
place, put up
*pōns, pontis, m. – bridge
poposcī *see* poscō
populus, populī, m. – people
porrō – what's more, furthermore
*porta, portae, f. – gate
*portō, portāre, portāvī, portātus –
carry
*portus, portūs, m. – harbour
*poscō, poscere, poposcī – demand,
ask for
*possum, posse, potuī – can, be able
*post – after, behind
*posteā – afterwards
*postquam – after, when
*postrēmō – finally, lastly
*postrīdiē – on the next day
*postulō, postulāre, postulāvī,
postulātus – demand
posuī *see* pōnō
*potēns, *gen.* potentis – powerful
potentia, potentiae, f. – power
potestās, potestātis, f. – power
potius – rather
potuī *see* possum
*praebeō, praebēre, praebuī,
praebitus – provide
*praeceps, *gen.* praecipitis – headlong
praeda, praedae, f. – booty, plunder
praefectus, praefectī, m. –
commander

*praeficiō, praeficere, praefēcī,
praefectus – put in charge
*praemium, praemiī, n. – prize,
reward, profit
praesertim – especially
*praesidium, praesidiī, n. – protection
praestō, praestāre, praestitī – show,
display
*praesum, praeesse, praefuī – be in
charge of
praetereā – besides
praetereō, praeterīre, praeteriī –
pass by, go past
praetextus, praetexta, praetextum –
with a purple border
*prāvus, prāva, prāvum – evil
*precātus, precāta, precātum – having
prayed (to)
*precēs, precum, f.pl. – prayers
prēnsō, prēnsāre, prēnsāvī,
prēnsātus – take hold of, clutch
*pretiōsus, pretiōsa, pretiōsum –
expensive, precious
*pretium, pretiī, n. – price
minōris pretiī habēre – care less
about
prīmum – first
*prīmus, prīma, prīmum – first
in prīmīs – in particular
*prīnceps, prīncipis, m. – chief,
chieftain
*prīncipia, prīncipiōrum, n.pl. –
headquarters
* prior – first, in front
prius – earlier
*prō – in front of; for, in return for
prō certō habēre – know for certain
prō hostibus habēre – reckon as
enemies
probus, proba, probum – honest
*prōcēdō, prōcēdere, prōcessī –
advance, proceed
*prōcumbō, prōcumbere, prōcubuī –
fall down
prōcūrātor, prōcūrātōris, m. –
manager

prōdō, prōdere, prōdidī, prōditus –
betray
profectus, profecta, profectum –
having set out
(tibi) proficīscendum est – (you)
must set out
prōgressus, prōgressa, prōgressum –
having advanced
prohibeō, prohibēre, prohibuī,
prohibitus – prevent
*prōmittō, prōmittere, prōmīsī,
prōmissus – promise
prōmoveō, prōmovēre, prōmōvī,
prōmōtus – promote
*prope – near
prōpōnō, prōpōnere, prōposuī,
prōpositus – propose, put
forward
prōspiciō, prōspicere, prōspexī –
look out
*prōvincia, prōvinciae, f. – province

*proximus, proxima, proximum –
nearest
prūdēns, gen. prūdentis – shrewd,
intelligent, sensible
*prūdentia, prūdentiae, f. –
prudence, good sense,
shrewdness
psittacus, psittacī, m. – parrot
*puella, puellae, f. – girl
*puer, puerī, m. – boy
pugiō, pugiōnis, m. – dagger
*pugna, pugnae, f. – fight
*pugnō, pugnāre, pugnāvī – fight
*pulcher, pulchra, pulchrum –
beautiful
*pulsō, pulsāre, pulsāvī, pulsātus –
hit, knock at, thump, punch
*pūniō, pūnīre, pūnīvī, pūnītus –
punish
pūrgō, pūrgāre, pūrgāvī, pūrgātus –
clean

q

quā see quī
*quadrāgintā – forty
quae see quī
*quaerō, quaerere, quaesīvī, quaesītus
– search for, look for
*quālis, quāle – what sort of
*quam – (1) how
*quam – (2) than
quam celerrimē – as quickly as
possible
quam – (3) see quī
*quamquam – although
*quantus, quanta, quantum – how big
quārtus, quārta, quārtum – fourth
*quattuor – four
*-que – and
*quī, quae, quod – who, which
*quicquam (also spelt quidquam) –
anything
quid? – what?
quid vīs? – what do you want?

quīdam – one, a certain
quidem – indeed
quiēs, quiētis, f. – rest
quiētus, quiēta, quiētum – quiet
quīngentī, quīngentae, quīngenta –
five hundred
*quīnquāgintā – fifty
*quīnque – five
*quis? quid ? – who? what?
*quō? – (1) where? where to?
quō – (2) see quī
*quō modō? – how? in what way?
*quod – (1) because
quod – (2) see quī
*quondam – one day, once
*quoque – also, too
quōs see quī
*quot? – how many?
quotiēns – whenever

r

rādō, rādere, rāsī, rāsus – scratch
*rapiō, rapere, rapuī, raptus – seize,
  grab
raptim – hastily, quickly
raucus, rauca, raucum – harsh
*recipiō, recipere, recēpī, receptus –
  recover, take back
recitō, recitāre, recitāvī, recitātus –
  recite
*recumbō, recumbere, recubuī – lie
  down, recline
*recūsō, recūsāre, recūsāvī, recūsātus
  – refuse
*reddō, reddere, reddidī, redditus –
  give back, make
*redeō, redīre, rediī – return, go back,
  come back
reditus, reditūs, m. – return
redūcō, redūcere, redūxī, reductus
  lead back
*referō, referre, rettulī, relātus –
  bring back, carry, deliver, tell,
  report
reficiō, reficere, refēcī, refectus –
  repair
rēgīna, rēgīnae, f. – queen
*rēgnum, rēgnī, n. – kingdom
*regressus, regressa, regressum –
  having returned
*relinquō, relinquere, relīquī,
  relictus – leave
*remedium, remediī, n. – cure
renovō, renovāre, renovāvī,
  renovātus – restore, renew,
  repeat

repetō, repetere, repetīvī, repetītus –
  claim
rēpō, rēpere, rēpsī – crawl
*rēs, reī, f. – thing, business
  rem cōgitāre – consider the
    problem
  rem cōnficere – finish the job
  rem intellegere – understand the
    truth
  rem nārrāre – tell the story
  rem suscipere – undertake the task
  rēs contrāria – the opposite
*resistō, resistere, restitī – resist
*respondeō, respondēre, respondī –
  reply
*retineō, retinēre, retinuī, retentus –
  keep, hold back
rettulī *see* referō
*reveniō, revenīre, revēnī – come back,
  return
*rēx, rēgis, m. – king
*rīdeō, rīdēre, rīsī – laugh, smile
rīdiculus, rīdicula, rīdiculum –
  ridiculous, silly
rīma, rīmae, f. – crack, chink
*rīpa, rīpae, f. – river bank
rīsus, rīsūs, m. – smile
*rogō, rogāre, rogāvī, rogātus – ask
Rōmānī, Rōmānōrum, m.pl.
  Romans
Rōmānus, Rōmāna, Rōmānum –
  Roman
*ruō, ruere, ruī – rush
*rūrsus – again

s

saccus, saccī, m. – bag, purse
*sacer, sacra, sacrum – sacred
*sacerdōs, sacerdōtis, m. – priest
sacrificium, sacrificiī, n. – offering,
  sacrifice
sacrificō, sacrificāre, sacrificāvī,
  sacrificātus – sacrifice

*saepe – often
*saeviō, saevīre, saeviī – be in a rage
*saevus, saeva, saevum – savage, cruel
saltātrīx, saltātrīcis, f. – dancing-girl
*saltō, saltāre, saltāvī – dance

salūs, salūtis, f. – health
    salūtem plūrimam dīcit – sends his
        best wishes
*salūtō, salūtāre, salūtāvī,
    salūtātus – greet
*salvē! – hello!
*sānē – obviously
*sanguis, sanguinis, m. – blood
    sānō, sānāre, sānāvī, sānātus – heal,
        cure, treat
    sānus, sāna, sānum – well, healthy
*sapiēns, gen. sapientis – wise
*satis – enough
*saxum, saxī, n. – rock
    scaena, scaenae, f. – stage, scene
*scelestus, scelesta, scelestum –
    wicked
    scelus, sceleris, n. – crime
*scio, scīre, scīvī – know
    scrība, scrībae, m. – secretary
*scrībō, scrībere, scrīpsī, scrīptus –
    write
    sculpō, sculpere, sculpsī, sculptus –
        model, carve
    scurrīlis, scurrīle – rude
*sē – himself, herself, themselves
    sēcum – with him, with her, with
        them
        sēcum cōgitāre – consider to
            himself
    sēcrētus, sēcrēta, sēcrētum – secret
*secundus, secunda, secundum –
    second
    secūtus, secūta, secūtum – having
        followed
*sed – but
*sedeō, sedēre, sēdī – sit
    sēditiō, sēditiōnis, f. – rebellion
        sēditiōnem facere – revolt
*sella, sellae, f. – chair
    sēmirutus, sēmiruta, sēmirutum –
        half-collapsed, rickety
*semper – always
*senātor, senātōris, m. – senator
*senex, senis, m. – old man
*sententia, sententiae, f. – opinion

*sentiō, sentīre, sēnsī, sēnsus – feel,
    notice
    sepeliō, sepelīre, sepelīvī, sepultus –
        bury
*septem – seven
    septimus, septima, septimum –
        seventh
*septuāgintā – seventy
*sermō, sermōnis, m. – conversation
    sermōnem habēre – have a
        conversation, talk
*servō, servāre, servāvī, servātus –
    save, look after
*servus, servī, m. – slave
    sevērē – severely
*sex – six
*sexāgintā – sixty
    sextus, sexta, sextum – sixth
*sī – if
    sibi see sē
*sīc – thus, in this way
    siccō, siccāre, siccāvī, siccātus – dry
*sīcut – like
    significō, significāre, significāvī,
        significātus – mean, indicate
    signō, signāre, signāvī, signātus –
        sign, seal
*signum, signī, n. – sign, seal, signal
*silentium, silentiī, n. – silence
*silva, silvae, f. – wood
*simulac, simulatque – as soon as
*sine – without
    situs, sita, situm – situated
    sōl, sōlis, m. – sun
    sōlācium, sōlāciī, n. – comfort
*soleō, solēre – be accustomed
    sollemniter – solemnly
*sollicitus, sollicita, sollicitum –
    worried, anxious
    sōlum – only
        nōn sōlum . . . sed etiam – not only
            . . . but also
*sōlus, sōla, sōlum – alone, lonely,
    only, on one's own
    solūtus, solūta, solūtum – relaxed
*solvō, solvere, solvī, solūtus – loosen,
    untie, cast off

*sonitus, sonitūs, m. – sound
*sordidus, sordida, sordidum – dirty
soror, sorōris, f. – sister
*spectāculum, spectāculī, n. – show,
   spectacle
spectātor, spectātōris, m. – spectator
*spectō, spectāre, spectāvī, spectātus –
   look at, watch
spernō, spernere, sprēvī, sprētus –
   despise, reject
spērō, spērāre, spērāvī – hope, expect
*spēs, speī, f. – hope
splendidus, splendida, splendidum –
   splendid, impressive
squālidus, squālida, squālidum –
   covered in dirt, filthy
*statim – at once
*statiō, statiōnis, f. – post
statua, statuae, f. – statue
stilus, stilī, m. – pen, stick
*stō, stāre, stetī – stand, lie at anchor
*stola, stolae, f. – dress
strēnuē – hard, energetically
strepitus, strepitūs, m. – noise, din
studium, studiī, n. – enthusiasm,
   keenness
stultitia, stultitiae, f. – stupidity,
   foolishness
*stultus, stulta, stultum – stupid,
   foolish
*suavis, suave – sweet

*suāviter – sweetly
*sub – under, beneath
*subitō – suddenly
subveniō, subvenīre, subvēnī – help,
   come to help
sūdō, sūdāre, sūdāvī – sweat
*sum, esse, fuī – be
*summus, summa, summum –
   highest, greatest, top
sūmptuōsē – lavishly
sūmptuōsus, sūmptuōsa,
   sūmptuōsum – expensive,
   lavish, costly
*superō, superāre, superāvī,
   superātus – overcome,
   overpower
*supersum, superesse, superfuī –
   survive
*surgō, surgere, surrēxī – get up, rise
*suscipiō, suscipere, suscēpī,
   susceptus – undertake, take on
*suspicātus, suspicāta, suspicātum –
   having suspected
suspīrium, suspīriī, n. – heart-throb
sustulī *see* tollō
susurrō, susurrāre, susurrāvī –
   whisper, mutter
*suus, sua, suum – his, her, their,
   his own
   suī, suōrum, m.pl. – his men

t

T. = Titus
*taberna, tabernae, f. – shop, inn
tabernārius, tabernāriī, m. –
   shopkeeper
tabula, tabulae, f. – tablet,
   writing-tablet
*taceō, tacēre, tacuī – be silent, be
   quiet
   tacē! – shut up! be quiet!
*tacitē – quietly, silently
*tacitus, tacita, tacitum – quiet, silent,
   in silence

*taedet – it is tiring
   mē taedet – I am tired, I am bored
*tālis, tāle – such
*tam – so
*tamen – however
*tamquam – as, like
*tandem – at last
*tantum – only
*tantus, tanta, tantum – so great,
   such a great
*tardus, tarda, tardum – late
   tē *see* tū

tēctum, tēctī, n. – ceiling, roof
*templum, templī, n. – temple
*temptō, temptāre, temptāvī,
   temptātus – try
tempus, temporis, n. – time
tenebrae, tenebrārum, f.pl. –
   darkness
*teneō, tenēre, tenuī, tentus – hold
*tergum, tergī, n. – back
terō, terere, trīvī, trītus – waste (time)
*terra, terrae, f. – ground, land
*terreō, terrēre, terruī, territus –
   frighten
terribilis, terribile – terrible
*tertius, tertia, tertium – third
*testāmentum, testāmentī, n. – will
*testis, testis, m.f. – witness
thermae, thermārum, f.pl – baths
tibi see tū
*timeō, timēre, timuī – be afraid, fear
timor, timōris, m. – fear
tintinnō, tintinnāre, tintinnāvī – ring
toga, togae, f. – toga
*tollō, tollere, sustulī, sublātus –
   raise, lift up, hold up
tormentum, tormentī, n. – torture
torqueō, torquēre, torsī, tortus –
   torture, twist
*tot – so many

*tōtus, tōta, tōtum – whole
*trādō, trādere, trādidī, trāditus –
   hand over
*trahō, trahere, trāxī, tractus – drag
trāns – across
trānscendō, trānscendere, trānscendī
   – climb over
*trānseō, trānsīre, trānsiī – cross
tremō, tremere, tremuī – tremble,
   shake
*trēs, tria – three
tribūnal, tribūnālis, n. – platform
*tribūnus, tribūnī, m. – tribune
   (high-ranking officer)
triclīnium, triclīniī, n. – dining-room
*trīgintā – thirty
tripodes, tripodum, m.pl. – tripods
*trīstis, trīste – sad
*tū, tuī – you (singular)
   tēcum – with you (singular)
*tuba, tubae, f. – trumpet
tulī see ferō
*tum – then
tunica, tunicae, f. – tunic
*turba, turbae, f. – crowd
*tūtus, tūta, tūtum – safe
   tūtius est – it would be safer
*tuus, tua, tuum – your (singular),
   yours

u

*ubi – where, when
ūllus, ūlla, ūllum – any
*ultimus, ultima, ultimum – furthest
ultiō, ultiōnis, f. – revenge
ululō, ululāre, ululāvī – howl
*umbra, umbrae, f. – shadow, ghost
*umerus, umerī, m. – shoulder
*umquam – ever
*unda, undae, f. – wave
*unde – from where

unguō, unguere, ūnxī, ūnctus –
   anoint, smear
*ūnus, ūna, ūnum – one
*urbs, urbis, f. – city
ursa, ursae, f. – bear
*ut – (1) as
*ut – (2) that, so that, in order that
*ūtilis, ūtile – useful
utrum . . . an – whether . . . or
*uxor, uxōris, f. – wife

V

vah! – ugh!
*valdē – very much, very
*valē – goodbye, farewell
vallum, vallī, n. – rampart
varius, varia, varium – different
*vehementer – violently, loudly
velim *see* volō
vellem *see* volō
*vēnātiō, vēnātiōnis, f. – hunt
*vēndō, vēndere, vēndidī, vēnditus – sell
venēnātus, venēnāta, venēnātum – poisoned
*venēnum, venēnī, n. – poison
*venia, veniae, f. – mercy
*veniō, venīre, vēnī – come
venter, ventris, m. – stomach
*ventus, ventī, m. – wind
vēr, vēris, n. – spring
*verberō, verberāre, verberāvī, verberātus – strike, beat
*verbum, verbī, n. – word
versus, versa, versum – having turned
versus, versūs, m. – verse, line of poetry
*vertō, vertere, vertī, versus – turn
sē vertere – turn round
*vērum, vērī, n. – truth
vērus, vēra, vērum – true, real
vester, vestra, vestrum – your (plural)
vestīmenta, vestīmentōrum, n.pl. – clothes
*vexō, vexāre, vexāvī, vexātus – annoy
*via, viae, f. – street
vibrō, vibrāre, vibrāvī, vibrātus – wave, brandish
victī, victōrum, m.pl. – the conquered
*victima, victimae, f. – victim
*victor, victōris, m. – victor, winner

victōria, victōriae, f. – victory
vīcus, vīcī, m. – town, village, settlement
*videō, vidēre, vīdī, vīsus – see
*vīgintī – twenty
*vīlla, vīllae, f. – house, villa
vinciō, vincīre, vīnxī, vīnctus – bind, tie up
*vincō, vincere, vīcī, victus – conquer, win, be victorious
victī, victōrum, m.pl. – the conquered
*vīnum, vīnī, n. – wine
*vir, virī, m. – man
*virtūs, virtūtis, f. – courage
vīs, f. – force, violence
vīs *see* volō
vīsitō, vīsitāre, vīsitāvī, vīsitātus – visit
*vīta, vītae, f. – life
*vītō, vītāre, vītāvī, vītātus – avoid
*vituperō, vituperāre, vituperāvī, vituperātus – blame, curse
*vīvō, vīvere, vīxī – live, be alive
vīvus, vīva, vīvum – alive, living
*vix – hardly, scarcely
vōbīs *see* vōs
*vocō, vocāre, vocāvī, vocātus – call
*volō, velle, voluī – want
quid vīs? – what do you want?
velim – I should like
volvō, volvere, volvī, volūtus – turn
in animō volvere – wonder, turn over in the mind
*vōs – you (plural)
*vōx, vōcis, f. – voice
*vulnerō, vulnerāre, vulnerāvī – wound, injure
*vulnus, vulneris, n. – wound
vult *see* volō